GETTING ORGANISED

A Handbook for Non-Statutory Organisations

Christine Holloway and Shirley Otto

BEDFORD SQUARE PRESS I NCVO

Published by
BEDFORD SQUARE PRESS of the
National Council for Voluntary Organisations
26 Bedford Square, London WC1B 3HU

ISBN 0 7199 1162 1

First published 1985

Typeset by D. P. Media Limited, Hitchin,
Hertfordshire

Printed and bound in England by
Latimer Trend & Company Ltd, Plymouth

Contents

Acknowledgements

The ideas in this book come from many people. We have both been involved with voluntary organisations for more than ten years – Shirley Otto as a researcher, and then as a freelance trainer and consultant in management; Christine Holloway in co-ordinating organisations and recently as a freelance trainer. Most of this book is the result of talking to people about their own organisations. Other parts have been adapted from books on management theory. We hope that you recognise some of your own ideas here too.

We want to thank everyone who, while working hard to make a success of running an organisation, allowed us to join their discussions. We also thank, in particular, the people who tried out the exercises or commented on the previous drafts of this book: Kathryn Davies, Landy Hashimi, Graham Park, Rick Skelton and Patrick Wright; and Di Harding and Karen Webb, who typed repeated drafts for us.

We are grateful for the co-operation of Bedford Square Press in the final presentation of the material and for their agreement that no objection would be raised to the reproduction of certain sections by bona fide groups for training purposes.

Finally, we want to thank the Croudace Charitable Fund's trustees for their enthusiasm and support, as well as a very generous donation.

WHAT IS THIS BOOK ABOUT?

The purpose of this book is to help you bring about changes which will improve the effectiveness of your organisation. The book is therefore made up of ideas, checklists and practical exercises for you to use. We do not look at what your organisation does, but how you organise yourselves to do it. You are invited to reproduce any of the exercises in this book for your own use.

We have written it with people who are working for small non-statutory organisations and self-help groups in mind, but we hope that it will be useful to teams within larger organisations, statutory or not, where people are expected to participate and co-operate in a team. We hope it will also be useful to members of managing committees. Chapter 9 is specifically for them.

Vocabulary

The vocabulary of organisations is extraordinarily confusing. We have tried to cut down on jargon as much as we can. We will be using the word 'users' to refer to the people who use the organisation. When we say 'managing committee' we mean any group which consists in part, if not entirely, of people who are not employees of the organisation and which has responsibility for employing staff or keeping an eye on the long-term progress of the project. The func-

tion of such groups varies, and the title can be trustees, board of directors, advisory group, executive committee, managing body etc. We have used 'workers' or 'staff' to cover paid and unpaid activists. Not all non-statutory organisations have employees: volunteers are workers too, even though unpaid, and self-help group members also are meant to be included.

We do not intend anything in this book to affect the role of trade unions for paid employees.

What is management?

When we say 'management' we do not mean 'the management', the bosses, senior staff or even managing committee. Management is a process in which everyone is involved.

Good management requires:

- establishing aims and making sure that there is agreement on the purpose of the organisation, its policy and its strategies;
- reviews and planning, to make sure that the everyday work is in line with the goals and policies;
- getting the necessary resources – money, ideas, time, talents;

> • ensuring that workers – paid or unpaid – have adequate training, know what is expected of them, are supported and supervised;
> • maintaining good conditions of service and working environment, including the legal obligations of all employers;
> • maintaining links with other organisations;
> • ensuring that the constitution or legal framework for the organisation is respected.

An organisation is a combination of elements: abstract elements, such as its goals and its methods of work; material elements, such as its buildings and equipment; and people. It is easy to think of these separately: 'It's a good project because it's got good workers'; 'We could do what they do if we had a new building like that'. In fact the organisation as a whole is defined by all these elements; and they interlock – if one element changes then the others will be affected. If the others do not adapt, the organisation as a whole will be strained and may even come apart in the middle somewhere. It is as if they were literally tied together with rubber bands – as one moves, the others must adjust or snap. Management is the process of making sure that the elements of an organisation interlock without strain.

Why are non-statutory organisations slow to use management skills?

This is not the place for a long discussion, but these are some points we keep coming across:

• The notion of management effectiveness is simply unfamiliar to people whose background is community work, self-help or social work.
• Some people cherish a myth that the voluntary sector works against impossible odds to provide a cheaper and better service than statutory agencies by using volunteer labour, with poor conditions for users and workers alike. They 'have a go', reacting to demand rather than planning strategically. Management skills don't fit in with this.
• The very way that government and trusts give money makes it hard for a non-statutory organisation to manage itself well. Good management involves drawing up long-term aims and programming development; grants which have to be renegotiated each year make steady work and progress impossible. There are also fashions in grant-giving: looking back over a decade one can see funding trends which are related to novelty or political expediency, not the greatest need.
• Another factor which hampers good management in the voluntary sector is the attraction of new sources of funds for very particular types of work. The availability of new money draws organisations into planning ways of tapping the new supply. This often has a lopsided effect on development; user need and organisational capacity take a back seat in the scramble for cash.
• The characters of some of the people involved can be a stumbling block. Everyone can be involved in high status activities – controlling the destiny of the organisation, making policy decisions, working at their own initiative to carry out their ideas and test their theories. This – in itself a good thing – has, as a consequence, the 'entrepreneurial syndrome'. Non-statutory organisations can be founded by individuals who want power, who might have founded an industrial empire in the nineteenth century. If an organisation is in the stranglehold of a charismatic

entrepreneurial founder, it needs a good structure to fight back. But the people involved are not likely to be attracted by 'bureaucracy'.

- Some people reject the idea of management techniques. They are seen as essentially flawed or dangerous, not to be used in an organisation which aims to empower people rather than make a profit regardless.

Can management skills be useful?

It is important to be selective about organisational theory and research and to check that there are no hidden assumptions about working styles or values. But the functions required in an effective organisation are often the same in industry and in non-statutory agencies. The difference lies in who carries out these functions, and what the organisation exists for.

Profit-making organisations developed organisational theories to make them more efficient at making a profit. We believe that non-profit-making organisations can learn from these theories to help themselves use their resources more efficiently too. The aim is different but some of the methods can be similar. An organisation which does not make the best use of its resources wastes not only money, but also the enthusiasm, time and self-respect of the people involved.

It is a rueful joke that new workers introduce new styles of working and even change the entire purpose of an organisation (sometimes without realising they have done so). But the opposite is also true. A change in working methods will affect the workers; a change in the building will affect working methods, and then even the organisation's aims. By viewing the project as an organisation we hope that it will be possible to decide on the form that each of these elements should take without forgetting that each influences the rest. They must be consistent with each other. They must also all exist. An organisation with no place to work from is obviously in difficulties. An organisation with no aims to work for is in just as much trouble. The problem is that we can all see that there is no *place*, but the lack of *aims* can be masked by enthusiastic people. If an organisation collapses when the founder leaves, then it had no aims – or the aims were inconsistent with the other elements of the organisation. If workers – or users – do not stay long then there is a fault in the structure of the organisation somewhere – it cannot be a run of bad luck if it keeps on happening. The chances are that the aims are unrealistic for those users, or those working methods, or that building.

In order to survive, any organisation needs to get the balance right between 'innovating' and 'maintaining'; between introducing new ideas and keeping up the good things from the past. Doing the filing is part of maintaining the smooth running of the organisation and ensuring that the past is not lost. Working out a new regime for the day's activities is, obviously, innovative. If the balance between the two is lopsided the organisation is in trouble. An organisation which is too busy maintaining the status quo to be bothered with thinking up new approaches stagnates and dies. It cannot adapt to changing circumstances. But small non-statutory organisations tend to swing the other way. Too much innovation with too little maintenance means

3

that an organisation does not learn from experience. It is perpetually 'rediscovering the wheel' because when it was invented no-one thought to make a note of how it was done. An organisation must have a structure which includes routine procedures to prevent this.

This book tackles questions such as defining aims, working methods and staffing requirements – and making sure that these are consistent with each other. Then there is the need to make sure that the organisation functions efficiently on a day-to-day level – that problems are solved sensibly, decisions made properly and carried out well. Techniques and systems need to be agreed so that everyone involved – workers, volunteers, users and managing committee – can work together for the benefit of the organisation and its users. Lastly the book looks at how you can check that what is actually going on is what is meant to be going on and if not, how you can review your aims, goals or methods of work.

HOW TO USE THIS BOOK

2

This book is a tool for you to use. At the end of this chapter is a list of questions. From your replies you will be guided to the chapters which would be most relevant to you.

Each chapter contains ideas and exercises to help each organisation solve its own problems. No outsider, whether author or consultant, has the answers to your questions. You get out of it what you put in. For example, if you dare not mention the difficulty which fills your mind and nags your conscience, do not blame the exercise for not providing the cure! If the group has not chosen to co-operate in doing the exercise – or has chosen not to co-operate – the most wonderful exercise will lead to nothing.

A word of warning. If you decide to use any of these exercises, be sure to decide before you begin what authority the group has which is involved in carrying out the exercise. If, for example, the group agrees that the aims of the organisation must be changed, has the group the authority to change them? If not, to whom must it take a recommendation? And is that recommendation likely to be acceptable to others who have not been involved in the discussions and experiences which led to the proposed change? Perhaps it would be better to repeat the exercise with them, as a way of presenting the recommendation to them.

The people who have the power to bring about changes in any organisation may be obvious or not. In some cases, an organisation has a very clear hierarchy and decisions cannot be made without formal discussion – for example, by a general meeting, or by the board of directors. In other cases, the formal authority to make decisions will be unclear. Even when the formal authority is clear, that may not be the real seat of power – perhaps the board of directors is always hoodwinked by certain workers. Or, more realistically, there are different seats of power. The formal authorities can prevent a decision from being taken; but equally, once a decision has been made, those responsible for carrying it out have the power to prevent it from being implemented if they do not support it.

These are ideas and exercises to bring about successful change. It is a waste of time, therefore, if they are not welcomed by the people who have the power to make those changes – whether those people are the formal authority or the people who have to carry out the decisions.

We would emphatically dissuade any reader of this book who has a position of power or authority within an organisation from using it to force the others to carry out these exercises – and this dissuasion is intended equally for members of managing committees and enthusiastic workers. For the same reason, we would suggest that if you do agree to try some of the exercises with an outsider to facilitate discussions (see Chapter 11), it is essential that those who have the power or authority to carry out any changes proposed feel involved with the results of the work.

If the members of a group do not know each other well or are tense or threatened, it is advisable to begin gently. There are many facilitating techniques and exercises to put groups at ease and encourage people to talk. They fall outside the scope of this book, but we have included references in the booklist.

We do not pretend that every problem which an organisation faces can be reduced to poor administrative technique, or inefficiency in setting aims or making decisions and acting on them. In some cases the more you investigate a problem, the more insoluble it becomes because there is an irreconcilable conflict of ideals or emotions. We hope that with the help of this book, it will be easier to spot which conflicts can be resolved and which cannot.

How long will it take?

Formal exercises take up a lot of time. Can a busy organisation spend so long 'gazing at its navel'? All the exercises have been used and proved useful. We have given an estimate of how long each exercise takes. The larger the group, the longer it takes. Each exercise can, of course, be used on its own. You may decide to review the whole organisation from top to bottom, by working through the book. If so, you will need to set aside perhaps a day a week for six to eight weeks, or a whole week while other work is suspended.

None of the exercises or techniques is sacred. Adapt them, use them in part or whole to suit your situation.

It will help your discussions if you appoint someone to chair. It often helps to keep a record as you go along, by writing ideas, decisions and tasks on to a blackboard or wall chart for everyone to see – so get large pieces of paper and some cheap felt-tip pens. Lining wallpaper is as good as flipcharts.

Questionnaire – where do I start?

To help you find out where your organisation needs to start, here is a questionnaire. The more people in your organisation who supply answers, the more interesting you will find the results.

Aims and methods – what are we trying to do?

- Is there any record of the organisation's aims?
- Could someone hearing them for the first time correctly guess what actually goes on?
- Does your work programme relate to the aims?
- When were the methods of work last reviewed, and by whom?

These questions are discussed in Chapter 3.

Monitoring – are we doing what we planned to do?

- Do you review how successful your work is?
- Do you know why you keep the records you do?

These questions are discussed in Chapter 4.

Roles – who does what?

- Do you ever feel put upon?
- Do you know whose responsibility each job is?
- Does everyone forget to take out the empty milk bottles?

These questions are discussed in Chapter 5.

Teamwork

- Is morale low?
- Do you work well together?
- Can you criticise each other constructively?

These questions are discussed in Chapter 6.

How to solve problems and make decisions

- Do you discuss the same problems time and again?
- Are decisions made and never carried out?
- Do you know who should make any specific decisions – for example, who can decide to close for a week's springcleaning?
- Can you set priorities for action?

These questions are discussed in Chapter 7.

Making meetings efficient

- Do your meetings last for hours?
- Do people get so bored they stop coming?
- Do you forget what happened last time, and why you are here this time?

These questions are discussed in Chapter 8.

Accountability and managing committees

- Do users of the organisation have power over its work?
- Does the local community have a voice?
- Do people know the duties and responsibilities of the committee?
- Who can call a committee meeting? Who can cancel one?
- How does someone stop being on the committee?

These questions are discussed in Chapter 9.

Avoiding isolation

- Do you have a handout to explain what you do?
- Do you have regular contact with the local community?

These questions are discussed in Chapter 10.

AIMS AND METHODS – WHAT ARE WE TRYING TO DO?

3

'Would you tell me please, which way
I ought to go from here?'
'That depends a good deal on where
you want to get to', said the cat.
'I don't much care where –', said Alice.
'Then it doesn't matter which way you
go', said the cat. . . .'
(*Alice in Wonderland*, by Lewis Carroll)

It is *essential* for an organisation to have a statement of its aims. This statement must be clear, so that it can be used. It must be well known within the organisation, so that everyone can refer to it to see how things are going. It must be accepted by all those who are responsible for making sure that it is carried out, including volunteers, workers and users. Lastly, the aims must be regularly reviewed in case the need has changed.

Why is it so essential to have clear aims? Without aims, it is impossible to decide on the means – in other words, if you do not know what you are trying to do, how can you decide what the day-to-day work should be?

If an organisation does not know what it *wants* to achieve it cannot check if it is doing it. Yet such evaluation is the only way to assess the organisation's work – it is not enough to *believe* that good is being achieved. Maybe your heart is in the right place – but you might still be putting your energy into the wrong one.

Perhaps it is important that your organisation can respond to immediate demands so you feel that you do not need aims. It would be better to have 'responding to demand' as an aim. Without a clear idea of what you are trying to do it is difficult to make plans for the future. When working methods are settled as you go along, but never laid down, it is impossible to ensure that the workers and managing committee members are consistent from one time or one person to another. Such inconsistency can be very harmful, especially if people – workers or users – are already confused and uncertain.

Certainty about aims has an important effect on morale and on people's commitment. When aims are confused in an organisation going through a bad patch people tend to assume all is lost, when a more objective assessment using the agreed aims as a yardstick might reveal positive morale-boosting achievements – as well as providing a basis for deciding how to improve.

How can an organisation set its aims? There are two basic types of aims, which we shall call the 'central aim' and the 'goals'. Different people use all sorts of different names – we have chosen these two because they are fairly straightforward.

These procedures outlined below can be used when an organisation is starting from scratch, or when an existing organisation feels that it needs to examine what it does and, maybe, reorientate itself. We believe that even when an organisation has a leader, these procedures should be gone through collectively by the group of everyone involved in carrying out the work to achieve the aim. It may be appropriate to involve different people at different stages – for example, managing committee members might be willing to let the workers settle the working methods – but we would prefer that people had the choice to opt out, rather than being prevented from joining in.

The central aim   *Time:* ½ to 1 hour

The central aim is the organisation's vision and reason for existence. To establish what it is, get everyone involved.

- Each member of the group involved in setting the central aim must spend ten minutes writing down a short statement of the organisation's aims. It can be idealistic, but it must also include definitions of the users, geographical area and so on. For example, if the organisation was founded to help handicapped children, a personal statement might be, 'To ensure no handicapped child in our borough is deprived of full legal and emotional participation as a citizen'.
- Each member should then read their statement to the group. It is helpful for one person to write up all the statements on a blackboard or a wall-chart for all to see. Anything which refers to methods should be left out. For example, someone might have added '. . . by providing playground, parent support groups', etc. This is a description of method, not an aim.

- Normally, the individual statements will contain overlapping ideas. Any differences should be discussed briefly. Some apparent differences between personal statements will be caused by misunderstandings or different ways of expressing ideas. Any real disagreements in individual concepts of the purpose of the organisation are potential causes of conflict. They should not be forgotten; record them to tackle at another time, perhaps using a technique for solving problems (see Chapter 7).
- From the individual statements the group jointly can compose the central aim. Make sure everyone has a copy. Write it on your noticeboard for visitors to see and participants to refer to. It can be a touchstone to test your behaviour.

Goals   *Time:* 1 to 2 hours per phrase

- The same group of people who drew up the central aim can best set the goals. These are the goals of the day-to-day work to achieve the organisation's central aim. If all the goals are achieved, so is the central aim.

- You must break down the central aim into its separate facets, since it will probably not be one simple statement but a string of key phrases. In the example given above for handicapped children, *legal participation* and *emotional participation* should be tackled separately.
- One person should write the first key phrase on a chart for all to see. Then the group asks, 'What would we see changed if this was achieved?' Everything you think of is listed at random below the phrase. The suggestions must be as specific as possible: they might be things the group would hear or even feel to be different. They must also be related to the central aim. For example, children coming here would play instead of sitting bored.
- When ideas run out, look for common themes in the list. Each theme can be expressed as a statement of an operational goal. For example, a social work project might find that the link between many items was that users' self-esteem grew. The statement would be, 'One goal is to raise users' self-esteem'.
- The individual ideas are tied to the goal by using the formula: 'One goal is to . . . which we will achieve by aiming for . . .' For example, 'One goal is to raise users' self-esteem, which we will achieve by aiming for more eye contact, assertive behaviour and more acts of initiative in our

users'. This is done for every set of items with a common theme.
- Repeat this whole procedure with each of the other facets of the central aim. The same goals may develop from different phrases of the central aim – this is normal.
- While you are developing the goals you may also discover that the central aim could be better phrased, given new thoughts and ideas. If so, amend it.

Remember – goals are *what* the organisation is there to achieve – the question of *how* comes afterwards.

The working methods

Time: 1 to 2 hours per goal

The day-to-day working methods achieve the goals of the project.

- The group which sets the aims and goals can continue on methods, or other people with practical knowledge can also be included at this stage.
- Using a blackboard or wall-chart concentrate on each goal in turn. Under each goal, list all the things people *could* do in order to achieve the goals. Many will already be accepted practice. If some things appear under every goal this does not matter.
- The next step is to cut the lists down to a manageable size. Which methods will actually be used and which will not? If the

priorities are not immediately clear, you can use a technique to set them such as visual voting. (This is described in Chapter 7.)

- The group now has a programme of action. Make sure that there are no glaring gaps. Is the organisation at least trying to achieve all its goals? If a goal is not going to be implemented in any way, should it remain a goal? Or do you need to turn your attention to resources, if you can't do everything you want?

- Check that the methods are consistent with each other and consistent with the central aim. For example, suppose that part of the central aim was 'to raise users' self-esteem'. From this had arisen the goal, 'keep the place clean and tidy'. If the group has agreed to insist that users scrub the floor as a method of achieving the goal, reassess whether this is consistent with the central aim.

A project which has followed all these procedures will have an integrated set of aims which paid staff, users, volunteers, managing committee and funders can refer to. From time to time the organisation can review its aim, goals and methods. Working methods should be reviewed once a year. At longer intervals it is wise to review the total organisation thoroughly including the central aim, goals and working methods. Perhaps there have been changes in the user group or in other local provision which mean the old aims are no longer relevant.

What it looks like

Here is a real-life, slightly shortened example of one organisation's statement of central aim, goals and methods.

Central aim:
- To improve the quality of the information and advice on housing available to people in the local council area.

Goals and methods:
- Goal: To offer details, advice and support on cases for all local agencies who deal with housing enquiries.

Method: We are available for consultation by phone three days a week.

- Goal: To provide information on housing policy and practice to all local agencies who deal with housing enquiries. Methods: We collect information from the Department of Environment, other housing organisations and journals. We learn local policies by monitoring the Housing

Committee and liaising with the Housing Department. We produce a monthly newsletter. We have regular mailings to a defined catchment group, including a copy of our newsletter, council leaflets on housing and free publications from other organisations. We publish occasional fact-sheets and directories of information.

- Goal: To provide information on trends of housing problems and gaps in provision of advice. Methods: We record cases which local agencies consult us about, to note where difficult problems arise or more information is needed. We liaise with the local advice planning group. We submit reports on problem trends to the local council. We support local campaigns by supplying information.

- Goal: To provide training on housing for workers in local agencies. Methods: We provide a programme of training sessions for advisers. We co-operate with training courses run by others to give sessions on housing where appropriate. We speak on housing to the workers at individual agencies when invited.

MONITORING – ARE WE DOING WHAT WE PLANNED TO DO?

4

To monitor an organisation means to collect information about it in order to see how it functions.

Monitoring means keeping in touch with what you are doing. It means that information is collected about the effects of your work. This information can be used to make appropriate changes to your organisation – it can form the basis for setting up another organisation – it can be used to raise money to continue the work.

It is not enough to believe that your intentions are sound and your heart's in the right place, and so you are bound to be doing a good job. Only by systematically noting what work is done, and comparing it with your aim and goals, can you *know* that your work is worthwhile.

What should be monitored – and why? Every organisation needs to be able to review who is, or is not, making use of its services, what form this use

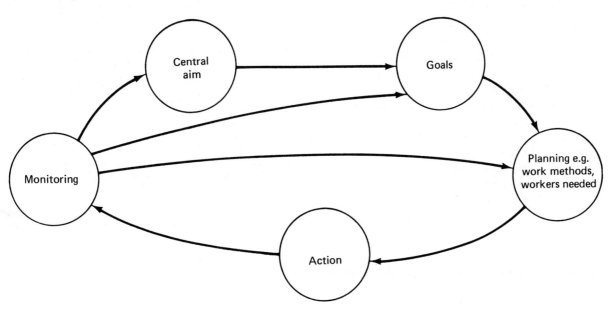

takes, how services are provided and what needs are not being met. What information is to be collected, how, by whom and for how long will depend on the type of work and the nature of the goals that have been established.

In effect the reason for monitoring is to ensure that it is possible to examine the relationship between present practice and its effects and that anticipated when drawing up the central aim, goals and working methods.

Often funders require details of the demands on services – usually termed 'statistics'. But any record keeping or collection of information should be clearly identified as intended to contribute to a review in some form of the organisation's goals and working methods. To collect information without a specific purpose is a waste of time!

Record keeping, 'statistics', log books or whatever are all means to check that an organisation's activities are on target. This is crucial to effective management.

Setting out a monitoring programme

The people involved in setting out the programme for the organisation should gather. (If there are more than six people, split into smaller groups.)

- The group (or groups) should decide which of the organisation's goals it wants to monitor. The group must state why it wants it to be monitored and by whom the results would be used.
- At this point, if groups have split up they should combine again.
- The group assesses each proposal for monitoring and asks:
  (a) is the suggestion clear, detailed and consistent with the goals of the organisation?
  (b) is the task involved manageable – is the information needed, for example, available without too much trouble?
  (c) will the information result in changes being made to the organisation?
- Dividing into small groups again if necessary, the discussion now covers the most appropriate means of collecting the necessary information to carry out the assessment.
- In one large group once more, the various options are ranked in order of importance.
- Decide and note what future action is required, of whom and by when.

A monitoring checklist

Any programme for monitoring should incorporate the following points:

Purpose of monitoring:

- Why do you want to monitor?
- What question is the monitoring to answer?
- Who is the information for?
- When will the results be used?

Procedure for monitoring:

- Precisely what information do you need to collect?
- Who will it come from?
- How will it be collected?
- Are the methods appropriate?
- Have you tested them to make sure they work? For example, is wording and layout of a questionnaire understandable?
- When will the information be collected?
- Who is responsible for collecting information from each source?
- Who will be responsible for storing the information as it is collected?
- Who is responsible for analysing and summarising it?
- Have you exploited all possible specialist advice and practical help?
- When will the monitoring method itself be reviewed?

Means and methods for monitoring

Information is the raw material for any type of monitoring. What are the facts? What have people involved in the project been doing? What has changed? Here are some ideas on how to get information.

Take note of unsolicited feedback from people who come in contact with your organisation. Do users frequently complain that you are never around when you are needed? Do referral agencies complain that you have not done anything for their users? Do funders turn you down because they do not understand what you want? Listen to what people tell you.

Before starting deliberately to collect any information ask yourselves:

- What do you want to find out?
- Exactly what are you asking?
- How precise does the answer have to be?

One or two simple but clearly defined questions asked regularly for (say) three months can provide information to add to the statistics in the organisation's record books. For example, the records may show that six users came to the community relations project last month after being referred by the local law centre. A phone call to the law centre might tell you how many people were referred but never turned up.

Counting

One of the easiest ways to get information is to count some aspects of people's behaviour. An attendance register with a few details about people is an example of a record. If one is kept, you can answer questions like:

- What sort of people use the facilities?
- Are they those for whom they were meant?
- How do different kinds of people use the services?
- Do people get a chance to find out all that is on offer?
- Do they come often enough to be able to make use of it?

All that is needed is a careful record of names and dates, together with any relevant basic characteristics such as nature of referral or age group. Simple counting can for example answer such questions as:

- Are all users in touch with a worker regularly?
- Are there enough opportunities for users to get counselling?
- Are there enough opportunities for them to get practical help?
- Is the community meeting really as democratically run as you say?

Questionnaires

A questionnaire is a systematic series of precise questions; it is not necessarily long or technical. It can be sent out in the post or someone can interview people and complete the questionnaire on the spot.

A questionnaire may be useful if the information you are collecting is to be strictly standardised. For example if you intend to publish a directory of facilities and need to ensure that every entry includes identical details. It may be useful if you need information from a large number of sources,

too many to be able to sort out the information you need from many individual letters.

Do not use questionnaires if the information is not readily classifiable, if the questions are not precise or if the formality of a questionnaire might affect the quality of the information.

It is absolutely essential that the questions are designed to get the same information from everyone. They must not be ambiguous – market researchers found there were over two hundred ways to interpret the question, 'How many magazines do you read a week?' Neither should questions imply the answer: it is impossible, for example, to say 'No' to the question, 'Do you think too much X is a bad thing?'

There are many pitfalls in designing and analysing questionnaires. It is a good idea to consult someone with specialist knowledge, so as not to waste time and effort. *Questionnaire Design and Attitude Measurement*, of which the details are in the booklist, can help you avoid some of the pitfalls.

Observation

One of the easiest ways to observe what people do is to count some aspect of their behaviour: for example, how often a social work client approaches a social worker for help. These simple techniques can provide very subtle information.

Here is an example where counting eye contact between people in a group monitors how democratic a meeting is. Eye contact made by a person speaking is known to be a good indicator of informal status in any group.

Eye contact

Time: ½ to 1 hour per meeting
to observe and record

This exercise is more formal than many of those we give, and may not be acceptable to all groups. For accurate results, more than one meeting of the group should be monitored. Be aware that the observation itself may upset the relationships: this effect lessens as the group gets used to being monitored.

One observer is given the job of recording eye contact, and prepares a chart like this:

Speaker's Name	Looks at ....
Sue	
Fred	
Ali	
Me	
Group	

The names of all the people at the meeting are written down the left-hand column.

When each person begins to speak the observer must decide where the speaker is looking. If there is clearly one person towards whom the speaker is looking, then the recorder puts the initial of that person on the line next to the speaker's name. For example, if Fred looks at Sue while he speaks the record sheet would read 'Fred – S'. If Ali spoke to Fred but did not look at him until he had almost finished speaking, the record would read 'Ali – Group F'. The important part is where the speaker is *looking*, not whom they are talking to.

At the end the observer counts the number of times each person was looked at. Those who were looked at most have the highest informal status in the group – they were the informal leaders *during that meeting*. This exercise can be repeated at intervals to note changes in relationships. It can be very useful to measure whether, for example, paid workers dominate volunteers in staff meetings; workers dominate over users; white people over black, or men over women.

An observer can also be used to count how many times people speak in meetings. Do some people speak more than others? Or some types of people, as paid workers, white people or men?

Records

Records are essential to everyday work. The one person who has all the information in his or her head – and not on record – might fall sick or go on holiday. Records are also essential for continuity of policy and practice in the future.

Nearly all projects have records. Some are clearly for practical use, but others have no clear purpose. Therefore they are often poorly completed and never used: a waste of everybody's time.

In principle all personal records should be confidential and should not be kept without informing the person who is being written about. Ideally users should be given the right to refuse – in practice, this may involve an unreal choice, and we should not pretend otherwise. 'Yes, you can insist we keep no records, Mrs Brown. But in that case you cannot take toys from the toy library, because we will not be able to get them back.'

Reorganise badly-used record systems by answering these questions:
- Why is this record being kept?
- Precisely what information must be recorded?
- What will it be used for?
- How will it be analysed?
- When will it be used?
- Who will be using it?

Review record systems regularly:
- What is being recorded?
- Is it being recorded thoroughly?
- Is it really useful?
- How do the workers and users feel about the records?

If the records are being kept to provide information for monitoring, set them up with this in mind.

A word of warning is needed if you plan to collect information and put it in categories. For example, an advice centre might decide to categorise telephone enquiries, and invent half a dozen categories such as 'tackling the council', 'housing', 'welfare rights', 'relationship breakdown'. It is essential that each thing can be put into only one category. For example, how would you record an enquiry, in our example, from someone who needs to get more housing benefit from the council after leaving her cohabitee? Everyone who collects the information must understand and use the categories the same way. To test this, get two observers to record and categorise the same event, two people to fill in the same questionnaire, etc. If they use the categories inconsistently, then the categories must be revised. Unreliable categories are useless.

Reviews

Reviews are a handy term for meetings where everyone shares and discusses their perceptions of their work, and its success over, say, the last year. Such sessions provide an opportunity for a discussion of feelings and intuitions which a formal assessment might not take into account. However, the disadvantage is that individuals' subjective assessment will be influenced by their morale, personalities, and prejudices, and an objective assessment might provide a very different picture.

An exercise for using goals in a review   *Time:* ¼ hour to set up.
                    As long as needed for discussion

Goals can be used to explore in a subjective manner people's perceptions of what the organisation has achieved.

- List each goal and the changes associated with it on the wall.
- Use visual voting. Each person has five ticks to allocate under each goal to the changes which they think are the most important indicators of progress towards that goal. The four changes which receive the most ticks for each goal are underlined.
- Set up a scale from 1 to 5 across the room, by writing 1, 2, 3, 4 and 5 on pieces of paper and spreading them in line across the floor. Each group member in turn stands on this scale to show the point at which they think the organisation is in terms of the four changes underlined for each goal.
- He or she then stands at the point on the scale that the organisation was at for each goal at the time of the last review.
- The changes and the differences in perception of those changes provide the basis for discussion – particularly if people feel able to move up and down the scales freely.

How to present the results of monitoring

Think about how can you tell other people in the organisation about it in a way that will enable them to understand it, and use it. It is recommended you consider:

- Who is the information for? How much background is needed? For example, if you are reporting to *everyone* involved with the organisation how many visitors come in, you may need to remind them which days the building is open. If you are reporting only to the full-time workers, they presumably know already. Figures which have been rounded up are easier to grasp. Tell them that there are, on average, 23 visitors on Mondays and 16 on Fridays. Don't bother saying that there are 23.17 on Mondays and 16.433 on Fridays.

- Have you made a clear distinction between your results and your interpretations (if any)? And are both of these distinct from any recommendations you want to make? People should be able to see clearly what the results of the monitoring are. They need to be able to identify interpretations and recommendations and may accept them or not.
- What is the best method of presentation? Many people are put off by long reports written or delivered, particularly if they contain numbers. Consider displaying your results on a blackboard or chart on the wall, or in the form of a model, a diagram, a dialogue or a 'play'.

If you are presenting your findings in written form, think of using pictures or diagrams rather than long sentences or lists of figures. For example, you can represent percentages in the form of slices of a round cake:

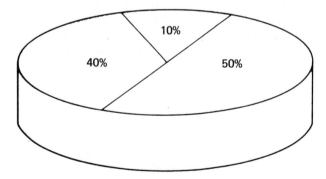

Letraset produce not only letters but also people, telephones, trees, scissors, etc, which can be used to show numbers:

- Have you summarised? It is often easier to understand information if it is summarised – for example, by making an average out of lots of figures on the same topic, or turning numbers into percentages. (If you use percentages, have the numbers available too.)
- Are tables clear? Leave out as much as you can, so that the reader can easily pick out the essential facts and not be distracted by a crowd of other details. Make sure that any tables clearly state what they are about, so that they can be understood without reading down the page at the same time. But it is also useful to repeat the points made by a table in words below.

ROLES – WHO DOES WHAT

5

Ever felt put upon? That you were being asked to do something which was not part of your job? That too many people were asking you to do too many things? Have you ever wondered whether or not something *was* part of your job? And are there some things which you cannot do because someone else is not doing their job?

Workers – paid or unpaid – and managing committee members often feel this way. The formal job descriptions which employees should get when they start work are not enough to ensure that everyone is clear about what can be expected from everyone else, though it is important that they exist. They rarely include enough detail and are often out of date. Moreover, volunteers, managing committee members and even some paid workers do not have them.

This section hopes to increase role clarity. By roles we mean the jobs each person is responsible for. We are not concerned about what might be called personal roles – for example, being the scapegoat or the peacemaker.

Establishing roles

Often people who choose to work for small organisations are opposed to hierarchies. They argue that if the purpose of the organisation is to encourage self-reliance in people who have had their confidence knocked out of them by their previous experiences, a strictly controlled work-force is no good example to set.

Research has shown that the more unpredictable and less routine the work is, the more independence must be given to the workers. Small non-statutory organisations often offer unpredictable, non-routine jobs, with considerable independence and control over work.

The flexibility of the work and the autonomy of the workers are attractive. Unfortunately this may also mean that roles become so ambiguous that energy gets wasted on unco-ordinated activity. Authority becomes vested in those with the initiative, opportunity or desire to take it, in charismatic leaders or in cliques.

Unfortunately the social status our society gives to the relative tasks of *bossing* ('management') and *serving* continue to influence the thinking of many workers in non-hierarchical teams. We are used to bosses doing high-status tasks such as making policy decisions. So everyone wants to get involved in this. No one wants to do low-status tasks such as filing, washing up and keeping the dust off the typewriter.

Low-status work tends to be involved in the maintenance of the organisations, and high-status work is innovative. But maintenance is as important to good functioning as innovation. Those who cannot be bothered to clean and file are saying that such low-status work is beneath them. Unfortunately this does not only mean that their position as defenders of non-hierarchical system is politically unsound – it also means that the organisation suffers. In a non-hierarchical organisation, all workers must do an equal share of the routine, boring maintenance work as well as the exciting innovative work.

It is important to be clear about two issues relating to roles. Is the organisation to be organised as a hierarchy or a collective? Are there to be any differences in the work which different people do?

Some organisations have equal pay and try to divide the work so that everyone has some low-status and some high-status jobs to do. In some organisations, it has been agreed that people do have responsibility for different areas of work, but that all tasks will rotate regularly so that everyone gets the chance to do everything. Sometimes complicated tasks are allocated to two people, so that the less experienced one can learn from the other.

In other organisations, people believe that any division of responsibility means that there is a hierarchy. This leads to a muddle where people are anxious. Some people feel responsible for everything; some things never get done. Resentments build up. This sort of confusion makes some people believe that only hierarchies are efficient.

We believe that the work of the organisation, whether it is collective or a hierarchy, suffers if it is unclear whose role it is to do certain tasks. Ambiguity itself can lead to the most complicated, high-status tasks accruing to the person who has the most confidence. So an unofficial hierarchy is born.

It also makes it difficult to criticise someone who has not been carrying out the tasks others thought she/he should do.

Sometimes each person assumes that someone else has done a task so, for example, the letters do not get put into the postbox for days. Or it can also happen that one or two people feel responsible for absolutely everything, with the result that they feel resentful that the others are not doing their share, and the others feel resentful that they are not trusted to be responsible.

An exercise for defining roles
Time: 1½ hours

Job sort

- Get the whole team together, and list on a chart in any order all the tasks which have to be done. These will range from the routine – taking out the dustbins – to tasks with much more impact – applying for the annual grants. (It does not matter if you forget a few.)
- In a column to the side of the list, mark the initial of the person or people who feel responsible for ensuring that each task is done.
- In the second column, mark the initial of those who last did each task.
- Group the tasks into categories, such as administration, domestic, policy-making, social or community work practice. In a third column beside each task write the initial of its category.

You now have a list of the tasks, their categories, who has been doing each and who thinks she/he should have been looking after each.

- Decide who *should* do each task and who should be responsible for making sure it is done. (This will often be the same person.) Remember it may be sensible to allocate tasks according to their categories; some tasks may not be compatible with others;

some should not remain in one person's responsibility for a long time. You also need to decide whether one person should be responsible for all tasks in one category, or each person should undertake some tasks from each.
- Repeat such a procedure at least once a year, and when new people become involved, in order to review how the roles function and whether they need adjustment.

Role conflict

Even after roles have been clarified, problems can still crop up. Just because someone understands what your expectations of their role may be, this does not necessarily mean that they can accept these expectations and the effect they have on their own job.

Conflict can take various forms:

- Between one person and the team – when one person cannot accept the others' expectations about his or her role.
- Among the team members – when people can't agree among themselves what to expect from a particular team member, it becomes impossible to fulfil all the conflicting expectations.
- Within one person's role – when one person agrees with others' expectations, but does not have the chance to carry out all the tasks which are part of the role.

An example of role conflict would be if one person was expected to write an article for the annual report while being expected to answer the telephone and casual callers at the door at the same time.

Role negotiation   *Time:* ½ hour

In cases of role conflict, negotiation is the best solution. Group members meet and send each other written messages which look like this:

To _____ (Name) From_____ (Name) _____

In order to help me do my job more effectively, I need you to do:

more of ....

the same of ....

less of ....

The message is about *tasks*, not personalities.

It would be acceptable to say, for example, 'I need you to do less opening letters addressed to me, because they then get mislaid'. It would be out of court to say, 'I need you to be less nosey into my business'.

Try to send at least one message under each category – more, same, less – to each other person. Do not overload them with information. Even if you have no message for someone in the first and last category you should still send them a message in the 'same' category – even if it just says 'I need you to do the same of everything'. Having filled in the forms, swap pieces of paper and give everyone time to read their messages.

In this way, everyone will get a clear picture of what the others think they should change in their role. You can discuss the messages, agreeing or, where necessary, negotiating. For example, one person might agree to open less post if other persons agreed to remember to open the post themselves.

This exercise can be used formally by a group, with a set time agreed for regular reviews. It can also be used much more informally between two people who think that it might clarify an immediate problem.

Putting things in writing guarantees clarity. Being specific eliminates fuzzy thinking, evasion through embarrassment, and future problems.

There are many aspects of employing people which are not covered by this book. Some are the legal duties of employers to their employees. Others are essential for good personnel practices, even if they are not laid down by the law. These are just a few notes – more details can be found in some of the books in the booklist.

Recruitment

It is essential to be clear what you are looking for when you take on new managing committee members, volunteers or paid workers. Identify minimum requirements before you advertise or ask people to join, and measure people against the requirements in order to choose among them. The minimum requirements should be drawn up with care to make sure that they do not exclude people unnecessarily – particularly to make sure that they do not exclude black people, people from other cultural backgrounds, people with childcare responsibilities, etc.

Induction

Good induction of new workers, volunteers or committee members is essential. Induction should cover the organisation's work and its context in the field. Plan for new people before they start. Work out what they need to know, and how you expect them to learn it.

Reviewing the work of new members of staff

This is a suggested procedure for reviewing how new workers are getting on.

The organisation will ensure that new workers get adequate induction during the first six months of their employment. Part of this will be three reviews of their performance. The aims of these are to:

- give the worker the opportunity to ask for help or training;
- give the worker the opportunity to receive constructive criticism from others in the organisation;
- give the management the opportunity to offer help or training if a worker's performance is not satisfactory;
- make sure that if work is totally unsatisfactory, decisions are taken after thorough discussion with the worker, colleagues and management.

The three reviews are held after 1–1½ months' work, after 3 months, and after 5–5½ months. At each review, the review group and the worker go through the checklist as set out on p. 26. They discuss the worker's performance, progress, training needs (if any) and agree on action to be taken by the worker and by other people in the organisation. The worker's opinions are given as much weight as other people's.

The first review group consists of three colleagues. One should be closely involved with the worker's job, and one should be as little involved as is possible in the structure of the organisation.

The review aims to offer constructive support to the worker, who is encouraged to discuss her/his strengths and anxieties.

The discussion is not minuted. A record is made of any action which is agreed, whether it is for the worker or for someone else to carry out.

The second review group consists of two colleagues and one member of the managing committee.

The same procedure is followed, with special emphasis on difficulties identified at the previous meeting. Once again, the discussion is not recorded, but any action to be taken is.

It is open to this review group to recommend to the managing committee that the worker's performance is unsatisfactory and that they cannot see any chance of improvement to an adequate standard. If this does not happen, the worker will go on automatically to the third review.

The third review group consists of one colleague and two members of the managing committee. The worker has the right to nominate another worker or trade union representative to join the group.

Checklist of topics to cover at a review

After each section of the review is completed, the group must ask, 'What action shall we take to help the worker develop?'

Individual job descriptions

- does she/he have the skills needed to carry out their tasks?
- does she/he have the capacity and opportunity to learn skills she/he does not have?
- does she/he understand which tasks must take priority?
- how does she/he feel about her/his work as a whole?
- how would she/he like to develop?

General work

- does she/he work the right number of hours – not too long or too short?
- can she/he use office equipment adequately for her/his job?
- can she/he produce written work adequately?
- does she/he do her/his fair share of boring routine such as washing coffee cups, filing?
- does she/he share in planning, e.g. by contributing ideas?
- does she/he share the overtime and worry when there's an emergency?

Policy

- does she/he understand the aims of the organisation?
- does she/he know where her/his job fits in with the aims?

- does she/he understand the political context of the work?
- and does she/he have ideas on how the organisation should develop?

Relation with other people in the organisation

- does she/he ask for support?
- and offer support?
- does she/he trust colleagues to work competently?
- does she/he obey people or committees who make decisions – e.g. the worker collective or the managing committee?
- does she/he allow people who make decisions to know what she/he is doing?
- are there any specific problems relating to individual colleagues or managing committee members?
- does she/he have any suggestion for improving the structure?

Relations with other organisations

- is she/he developing local knowledge and meeting other relevant organisations?
- does she/he understand the nature of the relationship between other organisations and this organisation?
- is she/he developing links with statutory agencies and politicians?

Final round-up

- is she/he happy?
- is there anything else anyone wants to say?
- has a record been made of any action which is agreed?

Support

The people who run an organisation need support – not only the paid workers, but also volunteers, members of self-help groups and people on committees.

Informal support

The atmosphere in any organisation should make it easy for anyone to ask for support when they need it. 'I'm feeling nervous about meeting the Director of Social Services. Could you help me work out how I should behave?'. 'I'm worried about that disagreement – do you think I was being unreasonable?'

The chapter following has some tips about talking to others about their behaviour which might help here, too.

Remember the need for informal support when making plans about the organisation. If there is enough money for only one worker, for example, it might be better to have two part-timers. Then they can support each other. If someone's work is rather self-contained – for example, they look after the money – it might be best to make sure that their workspace isn't cut off as well. One black person in an organisation with only white people will probably need support by getting other black workers, or – if that's not possible – from black people in other organisations locally.

Formal support

It is the responsibility of the managing committee to be sure that employees and volunteers have enough support in their work. The committee may choose to offer support in managing committee meetings. This can be difficult, however – if workers are anxious about their own work, or upset about a colleague, they aren't likely to feel comfortable discussing the problem with the people who are able to give them, or their colleagues, the sack.

For this reason, some organisations prefer to offer formal support separately. This can be done by hiring a consultant to meet the people involved in the organisation for an hour a week or a couple of hours a month. Another possibility is to set up a separate support or advisory group.

Supervision

Supervision sounds like authority checking up on people. It can, of course, be used against workers by bad employers. But it can be extremely helpful. Even in non-hierarchical organisations, some people have more experience than others; some have more skills in one area of work, others in another. Sometimes people are responsible for each other's work – a paid worker may, for example, be responsible for helping volunteer advice workers get their facts on welfare benefits correct.

In regular sessions, one person can help another look at their work – at what they think they are doing well, where they feel dissatisfied with their performance, what worries them, where they need training, how they would like their job to develop. In this way people are helped to keep a clear perspective, and get recognition for their successes and the efforts they are making.

Job descriptions

One of the greatest causes of disillusion is not knowing exactly what the task is or how to do it. For this reason, all workers, whether paid or unpaid, should have a clear job description. It should include a description of the aims, staff, resources, management structure and lines of accountability, users and context of the organisation.

The remainder must give specific information about the role and tasks of the worker. Whenever possible this should include estimates of the proportion of time to be spent on each task. It must include description of duties expected of the worker as part of teamwork, such as 'attendance at weekly staff meetings'. Each job requires particular skills, experience and personality. These should be written into job descriptions.

In addition, job descriptions need regular review and updating. This means there is a shared understanding of who does what.

Of course, all employees are entitled by law to have a contract of employment, and nothing we say should conflict with that. But it is useful to add more information than the statutory minimum.

A job description which is clear and has been agreed by the organisation can be a useful basis for monitoring someone's work. It can be used to check how new people are getting on, by discussing each item to find out if they are learning how to carry out their tasks. If there is dissatisfaction with anyone's work – whether or not they are new, paid or a volunteer – a clear job description helps to sort out whether complaints are justified. They can be used to set targets for improvement, or to praise people for carrying out their responsibilities well.

Contracts

Paid employees, of course, have the legal right to a contract of employment which is written down. We would like to suggest you consider whether it would be helpful to have a written, though informal, agreement between other people involved in the organisation – an agreement which might be called a contract. It can be a great help for two people, or groups, to write down clearly what they expect of each other. Such a contract may be developed between workers and users, members of managing committees and people who are involved in an organisation to define the duties and responsibilities of committee members as well as employees, between an organisation and its volunteers, or with outsiders such as a consultant or trainer. It is a clear concise statement of *who* will do *what* by *when*.

People can be unenthusiastic about making such a formal contract for reasons which we think are mistaken. For example, when new ideas are catching fire or a crisis is threatening it seems most unsatisfying to sit down and take the time to discuss and record exactly what is to be done. Such activity feels a waste of time, unlikely to ease tension or raise morale. Yet a group which does not agree clearly on what is to be done has chosen immediate gratification at the expense of long-term effectiveness.

People can also shy away from formality. A contract does not have to be written – though it is often more useful if it is, since it is easier to consult it afterwards. But it does need to be explicitly stated and formally agreed in some way. Such explicitness can appear unnecessary and too legalistic. People worry about putting things down on paper because it might inhibit flexibility of action, creative ideas and possible solutions.

However, to put things down on paper is to do more than fix them in the clearest possible way.

Such clarity is more likely to encourage new ideas than inhibit them. It encourages action to carry out the contract as well. The only flexibility of action which it inhibits is the flexibility to break the contract unaware.

The process of preparing a contract is as important as the end product. To get a clear statement means clarifying what people mean by the words they use. This helps to establish what they actually want, what is needed and what is possible.

This must be well done. Otherwise people feel let down later because what they thought would happen has not happened at all. You could almost say that it is impossible to overdo this part of the process. Working with people encourages the use of vague words (such as 'support', 'non-intervention', 'training'). Members of a group can each use the same word yet mean quite different things. A group which does not break down these vague words into details does not – and cannot – get down to brass tacks.

Discussion before the contract is formalised can reflect both practical and less tangible considerations: the price (if any); the amount of time each can expect of the other; the extent to which someone can be expected to become involved.

Participation in the process of defining the details of a contract leads to:

- The development of a sense of control and investment in what results.
- A greater understanding of what is possible. Many people need to be given permission to make demands, and need to learn what kinds of demand it is possible to make.
- A contract can be consulted when tension grows between the two parties. The contract is a statement agreed by both.

TEAMWORK – IS THE WHOLE GREATER THAN THE PARTS?

6

A team exists when people must co-ordinate their work to carry out tasks. The job itself requires interdependence.

This chapter shows how teams work more effectively if the members can manage the problems created by interdependence. Whatever the team's structure there are some common factors which will affect the level of team co-operation:

- Do the members share the same aim and goals for their work?
- How necessary is it for them to work well together to carry out their tasks?
- Do they feel a common bond and consciously see themselves as a team?
- Are some members more important than others – perhaps because they control spending money, or are treated with more respect by outsiders – thus creating a real imbalance of power in the team?

Members of a poor team fear and mistrust each other. They are bad at making decisions, apathetic or competitive about their work and leave their jobs frequently. They are off sick more often than usual. They are often too dependent on leaders (sometimes self-appointed) or in conflict over leadership. By examining how they co-operate or compete with each other, team members are able to stop feeling miserable and can begin to take steps to alter their own and each others' behaviour. By improving *how* they work, they do *what* they work at better.

How people behave in teams

Whether we consider a team in a meeting, or in the daily routine, we can usefully divide the behaviour of team members into three categories. These are *task-centred* behaviour, *group-centred* behaviour and *self-centred* behaviour. (We have taken these categories from research on people working together.) The balance between these types of behaviour will be different from one day to the next. It needs to be different, sometimes, for different tasks.

A team is never static, and good teamwork is not something which can be achieved and crossed off the list – it has to be worked at.

Task-centred behaviour helps the team carry out its tasks and consists of:
- initiating, e.g. proposing aims, defining problems, suggesting ideas or ways of doing things;
- seeking information, opinions or ideas;
- giving information, opinions or ideas;
- clarifying or elaborating to clear up confusion, define terms, interpret or expand ideas;

- summarising by putting ideas together, offering a conclusion to the group;
- checking that everyone agrees with a conclusion.

People-centred behaviour helps a group work as a team, bringing people together and making sure they feel involved.

It consists of:
- encouraging by friendliness and acceptance of others' contributions;
- facilitating others' contributions, e.g. by asking someone to speak;
- suggesting procedures which will encourage ideas to be shared;
- compromising by modifying one's opinion in a conflict;
- reducing conflict by breaking the tension (e.g. by making jokes), or getting people to explore their differences;
- listening carefully to others and not speaking unnecessarily;
- being aware of and mentioning feelings – one's own and others';
- testing that the team knows and is happy with its own procedures, e.g. for allocating jobs, making decisions.

Self-centred behaviour interferes with a team's work. It consists of:
- dominating to assert superiority;
- being aggressive by attacking or blocking other people or their ideas;
- drawing attention away from the task and onto oneself;
- forming a clique, an emotional subgroup for protection and support;
- pretending to speak for others as a cover for stating one's own needs;
- withdrawing physically or psychologically to remove uncomfortable feelings;
- acting the fool, messing about or making irrelevant comments to distract the team.

Self-centred behaviour is a danger signal: the team is not functioning well. Of course people in a team need to feel they are valued as individuals. When a team is working well and members feel they are a useful part of it, involved in the work and the decisions, they are less likely to experience the team as restrictive. It is when members feel the team to be too strong and feel overwhelmed and under-valued that they are likely to resort to self-centred behaviour.

You can use the following exercises at meetings to diagnose whether the team's behaviour concentrates on the task, group or self. Too little concentration on either the task or the group is as dangerous as too much self-centred behaviour. You can either tick when anyone behaves in each way, or note the individual person each time.

Exercise   *Time:* 45 minutes to record, 45 minutes to report on behaviour and discuss

Task behaviour

Initiating

Asking for information or ideas

Giving information or ideas

Clarifying

Summarising

Checking conclusions

Group behaviour

Friendliness, acceptance

Compromising

Reducing conflict

Listening

Taking feelings into account

Checking procedures

Self-centred behaviour

Dominating

Being aggressive

Drawing attention to oneself?

Making a clique

Speaking for others

Withdrawing

Messing about

If using the checklists shows that your team is not functioning effectively, this in itself may help the members improve. It becomes possible to draw someone's attention to the fact that they are behaving in a certain way once it has become a publicly acknowledged problem. For example, it becomes acceptable to remark, 'Sandy – you're messing about again now we've started talking about confronting the council'.

Each member of a team must be responsible for the success of the team. If one person is being made responsible for ensuring that members behave in a task- and group-centred way, or if one person assumes responsibility regardless, the remainder of the team soon abdicates responsibility and behaves self-centredly like a bored school class.

One can call each of the task- and group-centred activities 'leadership activities'. While a team certainly needs such activities it does not necessarily need one leader. With no leader, everyone must be aware of how their behaviour contributes to the success of the team. (Chapter 7 may be useful here. It discusses the role of a chairperson, especially in meetings trying to solve problems and make decisions.)

A temporary remedy for self-centred behaviour at a meeting is very strict chairing. Do not allow this to become routine. Serious investigation into the real causes of the problem is needed for a permanent cure.

Poor teamwork

Here are some suggestions to help poor teamwork.

Are team members overworked? Overwork often means that all decisions are made as quickly as possible, and members repress their differences to achieve consensus. Then people are likely to behave self-centredly later on – wishing to have their own way about something trivial, feeling depressed or alienated, or backbiting at the pub afterwards.

It may be possible to reduce the work load on individual team members. (See Chapter 5 on roles.)

For the team as a whole work programmes could be adjusted. There should be enough built-in slack to cope with emergencies – 20 per cent for 'Sod's Law' (everything always goes wrong at the most inconvenient possible time). Many 'unexpected' crises are not really unexpected. A simple example is writing the annual report, which, even though it is a regular necessity, precipitates a crisis year after year in many small organisations.

The 'margin for error' can be built in at the start. For example, the number of workers must be calculated to take into account holidays, illness and time off in lieu. To find out more about how to calculate staffing levels, see the booklist. Here is one real-life example we came across (with thanks to the nursing profession):

If 1 patient requires between 1 and 1.5 nurses, 10 patients need minimum 10 workers	10
Allowances for absence and sickness of 5%	10.5
Allowances for holidays and study leave of 10%	11.5
Allowances for maternity and other statutory leave of 2%	11.73
Allowances for extra work in small units of under 30 patients of 2% per patient (maximum 20%)	14.08
Total workers required – minimum	15

If none of these suggestions solve the problem of overwork, then the team simply has to decide what tasks to drop. If team members overwork themselves, they are helping no-one in the long run. At some point they will collapse exhausted and leave a disorganised mess for someone else to sort out.

These questions can help to set priorities:
- Which tasks drain energy because they are disliked?
- Which tasks would it make us feel bad to drop?
- Which tasks are least central to our aim?
- Do any tasks form a self-contained group, comparatively simple to cut out?
- Which tasks take most time for least benefit?
- Do we lack resources to do the task?

Racism means that black people's contributions to a team are undervalued. In some cases, assumptions are made about them because of racist stereotyping – what they really say or offer is ignored by white people. (This may have been formally identified by monitoring who talks most or is an informal leader, using the exercise in Chapter 4 – though the black people in the organisation who suffer from it know it already.) It is essential that every voluntary organisation with white people involved has a policy and a determination to tackle its own racism, as well as racism in the community. Part of this will be in recruitment and support of black workers and managing committee members. Another part is to make white people – managing committee as well as workers – attend racism awareness training. A third is to have a clear policy that no racist talk is accepted from anyone – even, for example, funders or users.

Sometimes *poor communications* make team members feel excluded. They do not know what other members of the team or management are doing, thinking or deciding. Tackle this by using Chapter 7 on how to solve problems and make decisions, or Chapter 10 on accountability.

If *working conditions* are poor – this includes physical conditions, terms of service and salary – morale is likely to be poor too. Low morale can cause a team to disintegrate, with each member behaving self-centredly. Strain can have the same effect. Loss of team members can cause emotional stress as well as extra work for those left behind.

Sometimes teams stop functioning because people *lose confidence* in the organisation's work. A symptom of this is gallows humour – team members make sick jokes about users and the team's lack of success. The best cure for this is to reassess aims and working methods (see Chapter 3).

Team members refuse to get down to a task because they are *afraid of failure*. They may be genuinely short of skills, time or money. Perhaps a short session learning a new skill together would boost their ability and confidence. Someone could be invited to come and teach the group, or people from the group could go on a course. Perhaps the group should face up to its limitations and cut back its aims – better to feel fulfilled doing a small job well than guilty for not doing a larger job.

Burn-out is another possible explanation of poor teamwork. After they have been in a job some time, people often start to behave in ways which are destructive to themselves, their colleagues and the people who use the organisation. This is sometimes called 'burn-out'. Here are some symptoms:

- Do you feel dissatisfied and unhappy without a clear cause?
- Do you see as little as possible of the organisation's users?
- Do you have a bug that you can't shake off?
- Do you refuse to respond to emotional demands while remaining blandly civil?
- Do you refuse to discuss new ideas?
- Is the awfulness of users the subject of many of the workers' jokes?

Organisations and teams within them should foresee the problem, and arrange ways of working to prevent it. People must be encouraged not to work too hard. They must look after themselves, relax in their time off and take their holidays. A rule that paid workers cannot carry over holidays from one leave year to the next is useful for this.

Regular assessment meetings can set goals. Success as well as failure should be discussed. Induction, training, supervision and support are all essential in minimising risks of burn-out. Job rotation and opportunities to use initiative to plan new developments can help people to keep their enthusiasm. Clear aims, working methods which are agreed and good procedures for involving people in making decisions all cut down on the stresses which contribute to burn-out.

The problems outlined in the previous chapter can lead to poor teamwork. Poor induction, lack of recognition of the need for support, inadequate supervision and unclear job desciptions can leave people feelng insecure and unable to co-operate effectively.

Feedback

Some of the problems of poor teamwork can be tackled if team members can talk to each other honestly and straightforwardly.

If two people talk regularly about the good and bad things each does, they can support each other well. Such 'feedback' makes us more aware of what we do and its effect on others. It makes it easier to change our behaviour.

Here are some ideas on how to tell other people about the effect their actions have on you.

- Comment has more effect if it is made at once. But comment at the wrong time can be worse than useless. So try to choose a moment when someone is able to listen.
- If you are afraid to tackle someone alone, bring it up calmly in a team meeting. You may find that other people agree with you.
- It is easier to accept comments about the way you behave if you do not feel that they are a personal attack. So make it clear that you are commenting on a specific action. Describe what the other person did, and tell them how it made you feel. Do not go on from this to psychologising about what sort of person you think they are, or why they behave as they do.

For example, say: 'You interrupted a lot in that meeting. I felt as though you thought I had nothing useful to say.' This is easier to understand, and cope with, than a general comment like 'You never listen to other people'.

For the same reason, give an actual example whenever you can. You might add, 'For example, you broke in before I'd finished explaining why I want a new petty cash system'.

- If necessary, don't be afraid to repeat the same message until the other person has understood. (Be like a broken record.)
- If you don't know whether someone has understood, ask them to tell you what they think you have said. If you are being told something about your behaviour, repeat what they have said to show them that you understand.
- Don't make assumptions about someone's reasons for giving you feedback. To explain *why* they said something does not explain it away. Perhaps they only commented because they were in a bad temper to start with – but they may still be telling you the truth.

Assertion techniques can be helpful if people have difficulty speaking up when others' behaviour is causing them problems. These enable people to believe in their right to say what they want without feeling that they have to be aggressive and unpleasant to do so. The booklist gives some further reading on assertion training. The role negotiation exercise in Chapter 5 may also be helpful.

Last resorts

All the suggestions in this chapter may not always be enough to rescue a team in dire straits. Feelings may run too high, the task becomes irrelevant in comparison and if it is done at all, it is not done properly. If all the team's procedures to carry out its work are adequate but are being ignored, while tempers are high or morale very low, it is counter-productive to struggle on regardless. The interpersonal emotions cloud the issues.

If this happens, the best approach is to stop work on the task and set to work to sort out what is going wrong. This means talking about it in a different way from that which is appropriate for a task-orientated discussion. We suggest that the team calls in an outsider such as a staff consultant for discussions.

HOW TO SOLVE PROBLEMS AND MAKE DECISIONS

7

To solve any problem you need to take the following steps:

1. Know who must be involved in finding the solution.
2. Define exactly what the problem is.
3. Decide what information you need before you can solve it – opinions as well as facts.
4. Find it out.
5. Make sure everyone has and understands this information.
6. Think of all the possible solutions.
7. Decide if you need more information to evaluate these ideas – if so, repeat steps 3 to 5.
8. Make a decision about what to do.
9. Act.
10. Assess whether the problem has been solved.

Defining the problem and choosing a solution are the two steps which seem to cause the most difficulties. The exercises in this chapter should help you tackle these steps constructively. But first it is worth considering some of the common reasons for things going wrong when a group tries to solve a problem.

What can go wrong

Co-operation

The group does not understand how to co-operate and needs to learn teamwork skills (Chapter 6).

Defining the problem

The problem has not been clearly defined. People can disagree about what the problem is without realising it. For example, the vague question, 'What do we do about our finances?' might be interpreted as, 'How can we cut future expenditure?' or as, 'Where do we apply to meet this year's deficit?'

Alienating people

The problem may have been defined in a way that alienates the very people who have to help find and carry out the solution. Perhaps the definition sounds as if it is prejudging the issue by using the vocabulary of one side: 'The do-gooders think that the local people from the community don't take enough responsibility'.

One very helpful way of defining a problem is to present several points of view. You might say, 'The problem is that individually everyone thinks: "It's so destructive the way everyone's split into factions – I don't belong to one" – but also believes that everyone else thinks: "Everyone's in a faction and that's the best thing for me to do too".'

Collecting information

Often the group has rushed into action without working steadily through all the stages of the problem-solving process. They forget to collect information; or sometimes, the people with crucial information refuse to give it to the group, for fear perhaps of losing power. Time spent on collecting and assessing information at the start saves time later reconsidering hasty 'solutions'.

Relevant information is not just 'objective facts' from outside, such as the bank statement, but also the attitudes of people affected by possible decisions. For example, to cut future expenditure a group home might decide that since food bills were high they would keep the larder locked. If this led to resignation by the cook or rent money spent on food the result would be a new set of problems.

Involving people in the right way

The right people haven't been involved in the right way in making the decision. A decision is ineffective if it is not carried out. If people misunderstand or dislike a decision they have to implement they will, actively or passively, undermine it.

In order to get the right people committed to a decision, they should be involved when the problem is defined. They may agree that the decision can be made on their behalf or they may want to be directly involved. It is useful to distinguish several different types of involvement. Not everyone who is *involved* in solving a problem needs to be a decision *maker*.

They might be:
> directly involved in making the decision;
> consulted; or
> informed.

To be directly involved means helping to choose the solution, and is appropriate for people who will have to carry out the decision.

Consultation has a bad image as tokenism, but done properly it is valuable. It means being involved when information is gathered – before the decision is made. The people consulted can contribute to an analysis of the problem, perhaps with facts, and/or offer reactions to possible solutions.

To be informed means being told about a decision in good time. Some people may not necessarily be involved in implementation of new decisions, but they nevertheless need to be aware of them. If you inform them before the decision is implemented you have the opportunity to say whether the decision has any consequences for them; and so they feel that they should have been consulted or directly involved.

Be clear what you want from people. Involvement can be overdone. A person who should simply have been consulted because of specialist knowledge should not have to sit bored and irritated through other stages of the problem-solving process. Alternatively, people who have been consulted about their feelings must be told that the power to make the final decision lies elsewhere, or they are sure to be upset if the decision reached is not what they wanted.

Is speed important?

Another reason decisions go wrong is that it is not clear when the decision must be taken, and how long can be spent collecting information or consulting. One end of the decision-making spectrum could be called 'quick' and the other 'thorough'. Speed is the priority for a quick decision even if this means that there may not be thorough fact-finding or consultation. It is not important how long a thorough decision takes to make, what matters is that it is based on top quality information and is accepted by everybody. Though beware of going on for ever collecting information and never resolving anything.

Here is an example. If the problem is 'How can we reduce the projected deficit for the next financial year?' a thorough decision needs to be made. If the problem is 'Will there be enough cash to buy this evening's food?' speed is far more important than consultation. If you are aware of the type of decision being made it is easier to be aware of priorities and constraints it involves.

Differences of opinion

Decisions may not get made because there is genuine difference of opinion about the best thing to do. If this is a division about the basic principles, it may be possible to resolve it by checking back to the organisation's aims (see Chapter 3). If, as is more likely, it is about tactics, there is no simple solution. Sometimes collecting more information about possible results of different actions can help. Often, however, division is caused by not clearly defining the problem at the start.

Decisions must be carried out

If decisions are not carried out, this often happens because there is no procedure for recording decisions.

It also often happens to teams without clear role divisions. No discussion of a problem should be considered complete until someone has been allo-

cated to manage the decision. The 'manager' is responsible for making sure the decision is carried out – not necessarily for doing it, but for making sure it is done.

Once you have chosen a solution, you must:

- List the practical tasks to be done.
- Set a date for each to be done by.
- Decide who is to do each task.
- Decide who will ensure the whole solution is implemented.
- Set a date to review progress.
- Decide who will record and circulate the minutes of this exercise itself.

Checklist for solving problems and making decisions

Use this to remind yourself before you tackle a difficult question or to work out why your meeting was a disaster.

- Was the problem defined very clearly?
- Did you decide what information you needed before you could make a decision?
- Did you collect that information?
- Did everyone involved understand the information?
- Did you discuss all the possible solutions before settling on one?
- Did you actually make a final decision?
- Did you make sure that someone was responsible for carrying the decision out?
- Was the decision recorded?
- How will you check if your decision was successful?

Decision-making questionnaire *Time:*
½ hour to get replies; as long as you like to
discuss them.

Here is an exercise to find out whether
people agree who should make various
decisions in the organisation. Everyone fills in
this questionnaire anonymously; though, if
you agree, it can be enlightening if they say
what their role in the organisation is. If you
wish, replace the decisions in the example
with topics relevant to your organisation's
work. Try to cover a range from the trivial to
the fundamental.

  Fill it in according to what you think *does*
happen. We will come later to what you think
ought to happen. Say who makes decisions,
who is consulted before decisions are made,
who is informed afterwards and who has the
power to stop decisions being implemented.
Here are example of abbreviations for groups
you might want to refer to:

W	paid workers together after discussion in a meeting
V	volunteers together after discussion
U	users together after discussion
M	managing committee after discussion
IW	individual paid workers
IV	individual volunteers
IU	individual users
IM	individual members of the managing committee

Write the names of any other groups you
think are involved.

  Use the replies to this questionnaire to
stimulate discussion and get everyone to
understand and agree where different types
of decisions should be made. You can see
where there is a decision-making vacuum
because no-one is responsible for something.
There may be a potential cause of confusion
or ill-feeling because two distinct groups each
have the power to make some decisions.
Perhaps different groups within the
organisation have different ideas about who
actually makes some decisions, or about who
should make them. Or maybe everyone
agrees who should make decisions, yet in
practice this doesn't happen.

Topics	Who decides?	Who is consulted?	Who is informed?	Who blocks?
Can users be banned?				
Which applicant for the job shall we take on?				
Should opening hours be changed?				
Should the headed notepaper be modernised?				
Should we talk to the press?				
What are our long-term development plans for the whole organisation?				
Who does 'housework' (like taking out the empty milk bottles)?				
What political attitudes are needed in members of the managing committee?				
What in-service training is offered to workers?				
What other campaigns or groups should workers be involved in?				
Does the place need a coat of paint?				
Are relations among people so bad that an outsider needs to be called in?				

Problem clarification:

'It always seems to go wrong when we. . .'

Time: 1½ hours

This is an exercise to help define a recurrent problem.

- Think of several examples of the problem which you want to tackle.
- Describe in detail how the problem arose – who did what, what came of it, etc.
- Pick out the recurrent patterns.
- Use your analysis of the patterns to work out exactly what the cause of problem is.

For example, 'It always seems to go wrong when we organise an outing for our members'. Describing the first occasion in detail, the group records that the first time, the outing clashed with the local football team playing at home; the second time, it was August Bank Holiday and too many people were away on their own holidays; the third time, the older people and the families with small children complained that they got back too late after dark. Using this analysis, the group realises that the cause of the problem is that the people the outing is for haven't been involved in choosing the date or time.

The sunflower   *Time:* 1½ hours

This is another exercise to define problems; this time between one group and outsiders. If the whole group is large it should divide into smaller groups to draw the diagram.

- Draw a circle on a wall chart to represent the group. This is the centre of the sunflower.
- Draw a petal on the sunflower for each of the outside groups the centre must relate to. For example, an adventure playground is the centre of this sunflower:

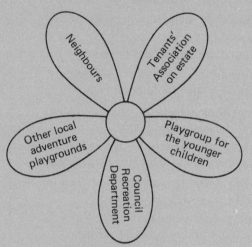

- Give each petal a score:
    - 1 = not many problems in relations between the centre and outside group
    - 2 = some problems
    - 3 = a lot of problems
- If the group split into smaller groups, join together now.
- Discuss what sort of problems there are.
- Define the problems relating to each petal clearly and write them down in a way the whole group accepts.

Brainstorming solutions

Time: 30 minutes to suggest ideas
30 minutes to make a consolidated list

Please refer to the list at the beginning of this chapter. This is an exercise for a group of people to stimulate new ideas and make sure they have thought of all the possible solutions to a problem before they go on to choose one (step 6).

- Go through steps 1 to 5.
- In a group throw up every idea you can on how you could solve the problem.
- As they come up, write them all on a list on the wall. Do not stop to discuss or comment on any of the ideas, though you may just ask for clarification if you do not understand. Never repress an idea because it seems daft – it might spark a brainwave in someone else.
- Do not stop as soon as silence falls. When the group has been silent for about two minutes, cross off ideas you all agree are ludicrous.
- Look for common themes in the ideas left. Make a consolidated list of similar ideas grouped together.

Go on to step 7.

Force field analysis

Time: 90 minutes

This is another way of stimulating creative ideas about possible solutions.

- Describe the problem in this way:
  (a) the present situation;
  (b) the situation as you would like it to be.

It is likely that there are some forces driving in the direction you want to go and others resisting. List as many as you can of both kinds of forces. For each problem take at least ten minutes for this step.

- Consider your list, and decide which forces seem to be the most important. Underline these. Indicate any which *you* can influence usefully.
- For each *resisting force* underlined, 'brainstorm' how you could reduce or eliminate the power of the force.
- Take each *driving force* you underlined and brainstorm the ways you could increase its effect in both lists. Write out especially promising ideas in a fresh list.

The idea behind the force field analysis is that you can get a problem sorted out better by decreasing the forces which oppose you than by merely increasing your efforts. The stronger you push the way you want, the stronger the opposition pushes back. If you reduce the strength of the opposition, your driving forces will achieve your aim more easily.

Evaluating solutions   *Time:* 2 hours

This is a technique to help with step 8 – making the choice among the possible solutions.

- Use the definition of the problem as a starting point. Write down on a wall chart, if you are working in a group, or on a piece of paper for yourself, what would be different if the problem was solved. Be as concrete as you can: ask yourself, 'What would I see that was different? What would I hear? What would I do?'
- List on the top of a separate chart or page, each solution you are considering.
- Delete any solutions which require skills, resources or time which you do not have and would not be able to get.
- Describe concretely what is likely to result from each solution.
- Compare each with the list you made describing what would be different if the problem was solved.

Visual voting by ticks   *Time:* 15 minutes

This is a practical way of making a decision – step 8 – without spending a lot of time on discussion if it is unnecessary. It does not persuade people to change their minds dramatically. But when not too much emotion is at stake, it is a good way to point out which choices are not strongly supported so that discussion can concentrate on the others. It is less useful when consensus is essential.

- List the possible solutions.
- Make sure they are understood by everyone.
- Each voter has a total of ten ticks to mark beside her/his choices. Some people may give ten suggestions one tick each; others may put all ten beside one suggestion which they think is vitally important. The items with the most ticks win.

Visual voting with your feet
    Time: 45 minutes

This is another way of making a decision – step 8.

This system is useful to involve everyone in making the decision and understanding the reasons in full. Getting people moving helps when energy is flagging because it all seems too difficult or it is just after lunch.

- One person volunteers to 'be' each possible solution.
- The 'solutions' stand apart from each other around the room. The voters go to stand beside the 'solution' they feel committed to.
- 'Solutions' and their supporters debate the advantages of their choice – those who are

not committed can move round, or join in the debate, as they feel like. Floating voters – and converts – attach themselves to their chosen solution.

Destruction testing

Once you have made your decision, you can use this as a final check before acting.

- Ask 'Who, or what, could prevent this from succeeding?' 'What would be likely to make that happen?' Don't forget that the group itself could prevent the solution from working. So ask, also, 'If we wanted to make sure our solution fails, what would we do?'
- Now list what the groups should do to make sure that these possible causes for failure don't happen.

MAKING MEETINGS EFFICIENT

8

Meetings are a way of solving problems and deciding what to do. Preparing the agenda is presenting the problem; taking the minutes is recording the decisions.

The style of meetings depends very much on the number of participants and style of organisation, so all we offer are a few hints. Details on how to run meetings according to company law, standing orders or the rules of debate are included in the booklist.

Preparing for a meeting

Have a checklist of practical details:
- Is the room booked?
- Are there enough chairs and tables?
- Will there be coffee?
- Can the essential people come?
- Who will chair?
- Who will record decisions (take minutes)?

Make people comfortable

- Get everyone tea, coffee or fruit juice.
- If people come straight from work, have sandwiches or biscuits.
- Make sure that everyone has been introduced to everyone else.
  - ask people to write their name on a large piece of paper on the wall;
  - ask people to prop up their name in front of them on the table;
  - ask people to draw a map of the room with their name where they sit.
- Never use initials which other people might not understand.
- Never refer to people who might not be known to people at the meeting without explaining who they are.
- Appoint someone at each meeting who will play the 'host' at the next – look after new people, make the tea, make sure that no-one is left out.
- Make sure everyone sits in the front row, or in the same circle – shy people often sit further back, and then no-one can speak to them even if they want to.
- Set aside a few minutes at the end of each meeting to say, 'How did it go?'
- Explain what you're talking about if someone arrives late, or if something is continuing from the last meeting which

some people missed – just as you would if someone new joined in a conversation in the pub.
- If the subject is dreary and boring, stop for a coffee break.

- If you've lost track, say so – probably other people have, too.
- Welcome people when they come – even if you just say, 'Hullo'.
- Say 'goodbye', or 'thanks', or 'see you next time' when they go.

Drawing up the agenda

Here is a checklist:
- State when and where the meeting is at the top of the agenda – and say what it is a meeting of.
- Ask people involved if they have anything they want to talk about at the meeting.
- Look through the minutes of the last meeting, and list anything that needs to be discussed at this meeting.

- Make a list of every subject which should be covered.
- Put it in a logical order.
- Work out how long the meeting can last. If there won't be enough time, what can you leave till the next meeting?
- Now you can start to make the agenda!

There are five possible reasons for an item to be on any agenda:

- to give information
- to collect information
- to stimulate discussion but make no decision
- to solve a problem
- to decide among possible courses of action.

Always make it clear on the agenda why any item is there – then even people who have missed the last meeting or two can prepare in advance, for example:

Item 1: staff report – for information

Item 2: Grant application – to discuss possible donors
Item 3: Job applications – to decide whom to interview.

It is not necessary to put every item that was discussed at the last meeting in a lump at the start of the meeting under 'Matters arising from the minutes'. It is better to put them on the agenda separately. Put them, and everything on the agenda, in a sensible order. If you must have 'matters arising', put it last.

Everyone who attends the meetings should know how to get something put on the agenda. For informal meetings such as weekly staff meetings, a piece of paper on the board where anyone can note anything they want to talk about is enough. For formal meetings such as managing committees, members must know whether to inform the secretary, chairperson or staff.

If people often have a lot of 'any other business', ring them first to ask what they plan to say and put it on the agenda. This not only saves time and confusion at the end of the meeting but also increases members' interest in participating.

Short items which are just for information can be written onto the agenda and not mentioned at all at the meeting; for example:

Item 8 – Date of next meeting – set already for 5.11.86 at 5.00 p.m.

Background papers let people absorb something complicated in advance and can save time at the meeting. But they are useless if they are not read, so send them out at the same time as the agenda – and make them easy to read.

Number each item on the agenda; note 'background paper attached' by appropriate agenda items, and head each background paper, 'Paper to accompany agenda item X for the meeting on (date)'. If people need to bring anything to the meeting, make it clear on the agenda.

Send out agendas, if they are drawn up in advance, in enough time for people to prepare themselves.

If someone is going to be asked to make a speech, give information, introduce a discussion or defend a point of view, warn them beforehand.

Take spare copies of all papers to the meeting.

It is encouraging to know when a meeting will end. Set a deadline. Ask people at the start if they have anything else they want to add to the agenda so that time can be allocated for 'any other business'. If the agenda is full, set a time for each item. Routine items need to be dealt with quickly, so the chairperson may have to be firm. More time and freedom for discussion are necessary for important new business.

At the start of informal meetings, or meetings where a feeling of commitment and solidarity is important, give the members an opportunity to review the agenda. They can adapt it if they wish. Once agreed there is a contract to carry it out.

Especially in fairly informal meetings where the agenda is not fixed until the meeting itself, beware of the tendency for people to interrupt discussion with new items which the meeting has made them remember. Do not get sidetracked by these. Simply add them to the end of the agenda and continue the previous discussion.

Chairing a meeting

We believe that it is necessary to have a chairperson for anything more than a very small, informal meeting. However, a chairperson is a facilitator, not a leader; nor should the existence of a chairperson lead other people to think they may behave irresponsibly. (See Chapter 6 for a longer discussion of behaviour in meetings.) A different person can take the chair at each meeting or for a series of meetings so that everyone learns how to do it.

It is the duty of the chairperson to:
- Explain the purpose of the meeting.
- Explain the purpose of each item on the agenda as it comes up.
- Make sure that the results of the meeting are recorded.
- Keep discussion in the right order. Information must come first – then as many ideas as possible – then make the decisions.
- Summarise every so often, so that people know where they've got to.
- Make sure that everyone has the chance to contribute.
- Make sure that a decision is made.
- Make sure that the meeting knows *who* must take action afterwards.
- Make sure they know *when* they must do it.
- Thank people for coming.

Meetings – or parts of them – have different functions. The chairperson's behaviour must adapt. When there is a potential for conflicts a relaxed style of chairing can defuse the meeting. A loose style will suit a small friendly group but will lead to chaos in a large public meeting. Urgent decisions require a chairperson who is willing to opt for decisiveness, whereas solving problems will mean encouraging everyone's brainstormed solutions.

The person in the chair steers the meeting. He or she uses the power entrusted to them to ensure the meeting runs smoothly. This is being responsible about people's time, it is not authoritarian.

A chairperson who arrives late, ill-prepared, confused or timid will lose the confidence of the meeting.

Provided the agenda has been clearly drawn up, a good chairperson should be able to control a meeting and keep it to the point. If people start to re-define the question or discuss the wrong question they can be reminded. But if the agenda is unclear it is not so easy to rule such people out of order.

As each item is discussed, it should be introduced. This can be very brief or very deep, and can be by the chairperson or perhaps by the organisation's 'expert' on that topic. Even the briefest introduction, such as, 'Let's go on to item six – this is to decide whether to close down over Christmas', reminds the daydreamers what is going on and the people who have not bothered to read their agendas are less likely to set off on the wrong track. An introduction also makes it easier for everyone to participate – no one need fear that they don't quite understand what's being discussed.

At the end of each item, summarise – 'Right then, we're agreed that Prabhinda is to draw up a draft application and will send it to me and the treasurers to look at before the next meeting'. This checks agreement and helps the person who is recording the meeting.

Make sure that everyone at a meeting feels involved. If people aren't sure what's being discussed, they won't contribute – or if they are afraid that everyone knows more than they do. That's why it is important for the chairperson to introduce each item. If people's suggestions are ignored, they will stop contributing. This happens to new group members, to women and to ethnic minorities, as well as to people who are personally unpopular. There are ways of recognising people's contributions. Refer to them by name: 'I think Grace's idea was interesting'. Even if the suggestion is impractical, recognise it: 'We can't do quite what Grace suggested, because . . .'.

Such recognition not only encourages the shy people, it helps bring out the original and valuable ideas which people who are not members of the 'in-crowd' often have to offer. And it makes the group's future stronger; people will want to come to meetings if they are valued and made to feel useful.

It should be accepted that it is the responsibility of everyone, not merely the chairperson, to encourage and facilitate each other. Sometimes, however, it may be best for the group to ask one person to be particularly responsible for this. If the chairperson has to concentrate on conducting business she/he may have no room left to check how members are feeling. If a meeting is likely to be very difficult, or if its purpose is not just to conduct business but also to have a pleasant time or increase group interaction or provide material for therapeutic discussion, the group may decide to appoint a 'process' chairperson as well as a 'task' chairperson. The process chairperson keeps an eye on the feeling of the people in the group.

Recording the meeting

Ask these questions:

- Was someone made responsible for recording the meeting at the start?
- Do you know who the minutes are for?
- Will they be able to understand what went on?
- Are all decisions recorded?

There is no need for the same person to record (take minutes) at every meeting. The task can rotate at each meeting, or even each item. Persuading the person who usually talks too much can be a good ploy to quieten them.

It is not easy to chair and write minutes at the same time; one person should not try to do both jobs. If you get lost while taking minutes, interrupt and ask the chairperson to summarise. No-one has been concentrating harder than you, and if you are lost probably everyone is. If your notes are illegible or confusing, check them with the person involved rather than making a mistake in the record.

Give each item a number, and a title which corresponds with the agenda. Record in a distinct way who is to do things – in a column at the side, after each item, or in capitals: 'ACTION – JO'. At the next meeting the group can check if things have been done.

It is essential to record all *decisions*. What else to record besides decisions depends on the purpose of the minutes. They may be simply to remind those who were at the meeting of the decisions taken. They may be to inform regular attenders who couldn't make it that day why decisions were made. They may be circulated widely to people who never attend, but who need to know what was going on. On the whole it is not necessary to record every detail of the discussion or to mention the names of the people who took different points of view unless people want readers to know what line they took on controversial issues.

A friendly discussion should not be recorded as if it had been as an angry row – the tone should reflect the tone of the meeting.

If events change after the meeting and before the

minutes are written, the secretary should add a note to the minutes, e.g. '(Since the meeting we have learnt that the application has succeeded)'.

Minutes should be produced quickly, then people can see what action they are to take in time to get the work done before the next meeting. They can also read the minutes while the meeting is fresh in their minds to make sure that it is a true record.

The minutes are approved as a correct record at the next meeting – or amended if necessary. If there are likely to be disagreements about the records, the secretary can keep his/her rough notes until the minutes have been passed.

Committees

Many of the practical details of a committee's structure sound trivial and to be concerned with them feels bureaucratic. Yet a group cannot operate without some structure; if it is not openly agreed it will still exist, hidden from view. Only those who know how the system works can use it. So make sure that it has been openly agreed and understood by everyone.

An effective committee will know:
- who draws up the agenda;
- how people can put things on it;
- who circulates it and when;
- who takes the minutes;
- who circulates them and when;
- who keeps a permanent record of all minutes;
- who calls regular or extraordinary meetings;
- how often meetings are held;
- how long they can last;
- what the demarcation lines are between this committee and any others;
- on what topics this committee must take the final decision;
- when it must be consulted before decisions are made by other people;
- when and how it is to be informed of decisions made elsewhere.

In addition, will there be sub-committees to tackle topics requiring expertise which occur regularly on the agenda and take up time but on which only a few people feel able to contribute? Finance is a typical example. If such sub-committees exist it is important to be clear about their relationship with the main committee.

Can the committee appoint extra members itself – 'co-option'? If so, can co-opted members vote?

How many members should a committee have? This depends on functions of the committee, and the size of the organisation, and how much time the members will have to learn to work together. Small groups can work together more easily, but cause problems when some members cannot come. Research suggests that decision-making groups of more than thirteen rapidly become ineffective as there are too many people for each member to keep in touch with. Unfortunately the more successful a committee is the larger it grows since more and more interested groups request representation. When numbers get too big an 'in-group' tends to develop, informally making decisions in advance. The meetings of the full committee merely rubber-stamp. (*Parkinson's Law*, in the booklist, describes this entertainingly.)

It is a good idea to have laid down a fixed term of office – the period that a member can serve on the committee without having to be reselected. Having a recognised period allows the removal of obstructive members, prevents an impregnable, self-perpetuating clique building up and permits members to leave without ill-feelings if they decide they cannot contribute any longer. Since good members are so rare, the efficient ones can be encouraged to start again.

ACCOUNTABILITY AND MANAGING COMMITTEES

9

In one way or another, almost everyone involved in a self-help group or voluntary agency has some kind of management responsibility – 'management' consists of so many separate functions. It is certainly not limited to the managing committee or the senior paid workers, if there are any. Making everyone more aware of the part they play in 'management' is what this book is about. But this chapter is directed in particular at the members of voluntary managing committees. Almost every voluntary body has such a committee in some form with authority to employ staff and supervise policy. We have used 'managing committee' to refer to these committees, though they have many names depending on the legal form of the organisation.

Organisations need to have a structure by which the people who are on the managing committee are answerable to others. They must not be appointed for life, but should have a set period of office. They should be elected or appointed by a group which includes other people, not just themselves; and which includes representatives of the people who use the organisation, other local people – perhaps those who might one day want to use it – and anyone else who may be appropriate.

There are also the legal requirements, by which the law attempts to exact some accountability over various forms of organisations. Charities, for example, are answerable to the Charity Commissioners; companies must keep company law and answer to Companies' House; trusts must have a trust deed; Friendly Societies must be accountable to the Registrar of Friendly Societies; and Industrial and Provident Societies have their own Registry. Even unincorporated associations are accountable to the law if they do not arrange their affairs justly.

In essence, the role of the managing committee is simple. The committee is accountable to the funders, the community, the users and the members of the organisation for the activities of the organisation. It must, in turn, hold the workers – if there are any – accountable for what they do.

But as soon as we start to examine what this means in reality, problems arise:

- to what extent can each group in the list hold the committee accountable?
- what if the groups don't agree with each other?
- what is the best way for each group to get itself listened to?

Accountability to funders

Accountability to funders presents tricky problems. It is clear that money needs to be accounted for. Books must be kept and audited to show that money has been spent on duplicating paper, not trips to sunny islands. But what if the funders also want to know what was printed on the duplicating paper? How much about the work do funders have the right to know? If the users remain the same but the political stance changes radically, do they have a right to be told? If the aims change from providing a low level of service to a large number of people to providing lots of support to few, should they have a right of veto? Or is this political interference?

When funders begin to talk about 'value for money' or demand evaluation of aims or methods, voluntary organisations become understandably suspicious. This can lead them to deny that evaluation has any value at all, or to deny that funders have any rights to examine how their money has been spent. Political interference is unacceptable and dangerous. 'Evaluation' can be an excuse for introducing change, or cutting off the money to organisations which are politically unacceptable to central or local government. This threat has recently faced more than a few national agencies, and is unlikely to ease in the present economic and political state of affairs.

Accountability to the community, users and members of the organisation

Who are the local community? People who are active in local groups – the Labour Party or Mothers' Union, the Boy Scouts or the Trades Council? Is it the people who never join in with anything, and still pay rates and taxes that support organisations? Or all the potential users?

The users of the organisation may not have the same interests as the local community. This might be because the users are, in fact, a minority. For example, a tenants' hall might be used by the men who enjoy the bar, whereas if it was used during the day for pensioners and women's groups, more people would get the benefit of the resource. It might be that the people who use the services of the organisation have unacceptable ideas about what it should be doing. Perhaps the current users of the hall argue against letting the young people have an evening of their own because they are racist, and think 'young people' will be black.

The users may have different ideas from the local community because the users are a stigmatised group, unpopular with other local people. How does a hostel reconcile its desire to be accountable to the community with, for example, the community's fear that people in hostels are perverts or muggers? What if the community wants the organisation to stop existing, and its users all to go elsewhere?

Perhaps the answer is to be sure that the managing committee is answerable only to the organisation, by having an official membership which votes each year for a committee. But who decides who can become a member? What if the membership is quite different from the users – so that a majority of men on the committee vote to stop providing women-only sessions, for example? What if the membership does not reflect the range of people in the local community – perhaps for example, some are automatically excluded because meetings are held after dark, when pensioners cannot attend, or in English, so that non-English speakers can't understand. Or if some people don't think of joining because they feel that it 'isn't for me' – everyone else who belongs is white/middle class/left wing/right wing/old/young/etc.

Groups sometimes attempt to resolve the dilemmas of accountability to different groups by appointing – or arranging the election of – people who represent each of the different groups onto their managing committee. The committee, therefore, includes representatives from local community groups, including perhaps political parties (or the political parties which are sympathetic to the aims of the organisation); users; local people or ratepayers; funders; and people from similar organisations with similar political or moral outlooks. Perhaps some places are set aside for women or black people.

Membership of the committee is one way to make sure that people from different groups in the community which the organisation serves have the opportunity to influence the work of the organisation and participate in planning. But by itself it is not enough, for any of these reasons:

- Perhaps the committee is a figurehead, and the decisions are really made elsewhere behind closed doors.
- Perhaps the committee doesn't deal with the items someone would be interested in.

  For example, a teenage representative from the Youth Scheme might want to help decide what sort of person the next youth worker would be, but that is done by the Interviewing Sub-committee which she is not on; and she does not know enough about council politicking to be able to influence a discussion on how to approach the Social Services Committee for a grant for the summer camp.
- The other committee members may all be skilled bureaucrats who prepare and read technical reports, run meetings briskly – and leave the representatives of the users or community out-manoeuvred, powerless and angry.
- Perhaps the workers refuse to allow the committee any power, manipulating the agenda and concealing real topics for debate.
- It may also be hard to get the user community at all involved in the organisation. Many advice centres, for example, are used only in times of trouble by individuals who never talk to each other and would not picture themselves as having a community of interest.
- Other organisations may be catering for a transient population, such as homeless people in emergency accommodation. No-one is around long enough to become part of the formal procedures for running the place.

In such cases, drastic changes may be needed to the membership and style of committee meetings. In addition, alternative forms of participation in management can be tried out. For example:

- A 'grievance procedure' for user members of the community to complain about how the organisation is run. This should be advertised clearly – for example, on a poster in the hall. It should make clear to whom the workers are accountable, so that users can speak or write to the management.
- An 'ombudsperson' – one member of the managing committee with special responsibility for liaison between the committee and users, or members of the community with the duty to ensure that their point of view is heard.
- A 'shop steward' – a user elected to speak for the others.

- A sub-committee of the managing committee with high user involvement and clearly defined responsibility for discussing matters of particular interest to users.
- Community meetings where everyone involved in the daily life of the organisation shares information and decides a policy of a defined type.
- General meetings every couple of months or every year, where anyone – users, former users, workers, volunteers, committee members and the community discuss the work of the organisation and suggest improvements.
- Open days, exhibitions, and so on. (See Chapter 10).

Managing committees

Whoever they are, members of managing committees find their role at times boring and at times baffling. Workers are at times exasperated by the apparent interference of committee members where they are not needed or slowness to offer support when it is needed. The committee has the power yet the workers have the responsibility. How can you improve the effectiveness of a managing committee?

What should the committee do, and what sort of people are needed?

Everyone must be clear what the functions of the committee are, what is – and what is not – the responsibility of the committee. The questionnaire on decision-making on p. 40 is useful in defining the responsibilities of a managing committee. It can also be helpful to write duties down clearly, even perhaps in the form of a contract (see p. 65).

Not all management functions have to be carried out by the committee. Some are legally the committee's responsibility. Some may be incompatible – if the committee decides to carry out one function, it makes it difficult for it to carry out some other functions satisfactorily. In such cases the committee may delegate to another body. For example, support of workers can be incompatible with being the employer who can hire and fire.

Although the committee is *responsible* for everything which happens in the organisation, this does not mean that it actually has to *do* everything. The daily work is rarely seen as something for the committee to *do*. Other functions tend to accumulate to the managing committee because they have to be done, there is no other body to do them and the committee is responsible for seeing that they are done: but they are not *necessarily* part of the committee's work. Our aim is to help your organisation use its managing committee in the way that makes the most sense.

As we have discussed, managing committees provide an opportunity for interest groups to participate in planning the work of the organisation. Such groups could include employees, users, funders, volunteers, other similar organisations and the local community. It is essential that the committee should reflect the ethnic make-up of the community, and should include as many women as men, to help combat racism and sexism.

It may not be possible in law for employees to be full voting members – this will depend on your constitution. Sometimes employees do not want to be full members of the body which has the final power to give workers the sack, for trade union reasons. The temptation to invite former employees to join the committee should be treated cautiously – such people tend to look back rather than forward.

If they try to exert any quality control at all beyond the annual audit, funding bodies most often ask for a seat on the managing committee. This creates a problem: the funder's representative is there to inspect and report; the committee exists to manage. In time of change or trouble, when good management is essential, it may also seem essential to keep the funders in the dark. This may be reprehensible, but it seems inevitable.

Another disadvantage is that because they hold the purse-strings, funders have final authority on all decisions: yet they are unlikely to be best equipped to make the decisions. On the positive side, funders involved on a committee may feel responsible for the work and so less likely to cut off funds.

The role of a funding body's representative on the committee needs to be carefully defined and agreed. Consider inviting the representative to join, for example, the finance sub-committee but not the full managing committee; or the full committee but not the staff advisory sub-committee where work difficulties are thrashed out.

In addition, do not assume that funders' representatives understand the management of voluntary organisations. Take extra care to explain their role, to try to encourage them to contribute usefully without exerting political control.

Managing committee members are often expected to have a more detached view than workers. Not being caught up in the daily business, boredom and breakdowns they have time to sit back and assess. They should be responsible for the organisational health of the project, for its aims, working methods and monitoring. Workers have to answer for their actions, not because the committee is 'the boss' but because in answering they have the opportunity to share responsibility and think things through. In initiating or taking part in reviews of past policy and practice, the committee acts as a sounding board for the workers to thrash out suggestions for change. The committee can plan new work and ensure that the organisation does not simply react to outside forces. Developments in the field can be taken into account, particularly if members of the committee have experience of related organisations.

The committee can also brake enthusiastic but ill-informed changes suggested by workers. Because of their investment in the project, workers sometimes cannot see the wood for the trees. Also, when staff turnover is fast the committee can maintain continuity. Members remember past developments and the reasons for them. This helps everyone to learn from past experience – we too often rejoice to rediscover the wheel – and also helps workers and users feel that there is a connection between the organisation as it now is and its past.

If the committee is to have this sort of role, it is wise to include some members with experience elsewhere in the field, and some with the skills and clear minds needed to cope with the abstractions of long-term planning.

People can be invited on to the committee because they have specific skills or experience which the workers cannot be expected to have. This could be simply the ability to tell the project what it is like to be a user, funder or neighbour of the project. It could be expertise in, for example, the law, book-keeping, fundraising, public relations and advertising, building or how the local authority works. Consider, however, whether it would be better to call in such experts when necessary, rather than making them members with full responsibilities. If you do have them, use them. Managing committee members are volunteers and need to feel that their time is well spent. If you need legal information, do not ignore the solicitor who has been attending committee meetings for years.

An organisation often needs a few managing committee members who can help foster an image of respectability, locally or nationally. But such VIPs are often very busy and are too remote to understand the work of the organisation. If you believe you really need to have notables on the committee, decide whom they need to impress and, if possible, choose someone who has other useful qualities as well. As tactfully as necessary, make sure that notables know why they have been invited.

As an employing body an organisation has legal responsibilities to its staff. The managing committee must ensure that these are carried out. There must be some formal structure for resolving disputes among workers, and between workers and committee. Any managing body should consult the trade union of its employees in setting up a grievance and disciplinary procedure.

It is worth considering whether the organisation would benefit from having a committee member with experience in employment, such as a personnel officer from industry, a local business person or a trade union officer.

The committee at work

To be effective a managing committee should have its functions clearly worked out. Each member must understand and agree what they contribute. This means the members of the committee must be familiar with the committee – its legal responsibilities, functions and structure; and the organisation – its aims, goals, method of work, and users.

The first meeting after a new committee has been elected can be a good opportunity to teach new members about the organisation, and for the whole committee to set itself a plan for the coming year.

Take nothing for granted. Even if committee members have known the organisation beforehand, they need to be introduced to the work just as much as new employees and clients. Without a firm grip on what goes on, how can they discuss policies for the future or fundraising.

A copy of the Trust Deed, Memorandum of Association or other constitution should be provided for each member. All those involved should discuss the functions of the committee. Once agreed, write these down for future reference. Do not provide members with a sheet of instructions. The purpose is to get everyone to understand and agree – which a sheet of unread or ill-digested instructions cannot do. The process of deciding is as important as what is decided upon.

A managing committee is a team with a task, and it needs a structure which helps it carry out its tasks. This book's chapters on team work, solving problems, making decisions and running meetings efficiently are useful to a managing committee as well as a staff team. In addition, decide how workers report to the committee. What are the staff lines of accountability – does each worker answer for him/herself, or is one worker a channel for all the rest to communicate with the committee?

The answers to many of the questions about the committee's procedures will be defined by the organisation's legal documents. But do not think, 'We don't need to discuss that because it's laid down somewhere in that incomprehensible document that we haven't got round to reading yet. . . .' The essential point is that everyone should *know* the answers.

Ensuring continuing good work

It is no good to sit back and forget about a commit-

tee once it has been set up. To make sure that it is functioning properly it needs regular checks.

Every new member to join the committee needs to be introduced to the work of the organisation and the committee, just as the first members were. Every time the committee comes up for re-election, or at least every year, the committee's work should be reviewed. Did it do what it said it was to do? If not, what needs to be done to stop the same thing happening next year? Were the members appropriate to the functions? If not, should new members be sought? Was the structure useful? Was it kept to?

A checklist for committee members

- Can you describe the aims, methods and user group of the organisation?
- Do you know the functions of the committee?
- Do you know the structure of the committee?
- Can you attend meetings regularly? (if not, resign).
- Do you read the papers you are sent before the meeting?
- Do you complain about the workers behind their backs or discuss your worries openly?
- Are you aware of any conflicts of interest which membership of the committee entails (for example, if you represent another interest group)?
- Do you adopt a special style of speaking at meetings, which perhaps sounds rather pompous?
- Do you treat the meeting as a competition rather than an opportunity to work together?
- If you disagree with a decision by your fellow committee members should you threaten to resign? If that compelled the committee to do what you want, would your position be tenable afterwards? If it does not compel the committee to change its mind, would your resignation do more good than your continued membership?

For workers who have managing committees

Managing committee members are dependent on workers for what they know about the project. If they do not understand what happens, it is the fault of the workers for not explaining properly.

Workers must make themselves accountable, to each other and to their managing group. They must hold each other accountable, too. If colleagues are not doing their job properly, do not work twice as hard to make up – ask them what is wrong. This is even more essential in a non-hierarchical team with collective management. If no-one is the boss, everyone must be.

Information is power. If you withhold information, you withhold power. Workers usually have most information and this means they must share their power by sharing information. They must inform users and they must inform the managing committee. Sometimes when workers withhold information from the managing committee, they make it impossible for anyone to feel the committee has the real authority to make decisions, especially those concerned with key areas like long-term planning, staff conditions of service, and conflict. The result is inefficiency, suspicion and ill-feeling. The effects can be disastrous.

A checklist on managing committees

At the first meeting of a new committee – for example, after the AGM each year – everyone on the managing committee and the workers need to discuss and agree:

How the managing committee will be organised

- everyone should have everyone else's name and address
- who takes the minutes?
- who takes the chair?
- when should meetings be?
- who do you tell if you cannot come?
- who has the power to cancel a meeting?
- who makes the agenda?
- how can other people get something put onto the agenda?
- when are papers for the meetings to be sent out?
- when are minutes to be sent out?

Responsibilities

- what is the managing committee's job?
- what decisions must the committee take?
- what decisions can the workers take?
- when must the committee consult the workers?
- what sort of things must the workers tell the committee about?
- how will the workers make themselves accountable to the committee? For example, will they produce written reports? If so, what about?

The programme for the year

- what are the overall aims of the organisation?
- what areas of work should be top priority for the year?
- what implications does this have for the work?
- what implications does it have for resources – people, money, etc?

Expectations

Time: 10 minutes to fill it in.
Up to 1 hour to discuss

Here is an exercise which workers and committee members can use.
- Each person should fill in their own requests in the appropriate column.
- The entire group can then agree what is reasonable to expect of each other.

What workers ask of the committee	What the committee ask of the workers

AVOIDING ISOLATION

10

We have been considering an organisation from the inside. All these techniques are tools to get the organisation working well. But an organisation does not exist in isolation from the environment.

Some environmental influences are direct and obvious. For example, a shortage of money or the funder's enthusiasms may affect an organisation. It may mean that new schemes are invented, not because they are urgently needed, but because they have a good chance of attracting funds.

Other outside influences are subtler and more far-reaching. An organisation may not be much respected if its users are generally not much respected in the locality or in wider society. The attitudes of society will tend to influence people's view of themselves. The attitudes of the workers are influenced too. They may agree with prejudice. They can also be so eager to reject society's prejudices that they lose a realistic assessment of the situation.

To work out the influence which outside factors have on the project use the 'sunflower' technique described in Chapter 7.

Keep in touch

It is essential for an organisation to be able to adapt to a changing environment. The more turbulent the environment, the more adaptable you must be. What outside factors could change and affect your work?

Has the law been changed? For example, new welfare benefit regulations might affect a self-help group of single parents. A change in local facilities may affect your organisation – even something as elementary as changing opening hours. So might changes in people's habits. For instance, drug users tend to follow fashions in drug abuse and a project to help drug addicts would have to adapt its referral criteria as fashions change.

A change in wider social attitudes may be crucial. A nineteenth-century charity may have been set up to help 'fallen women' by getting them good jobs as servants. Such an organisation would find itself high and dry today unless it brought its aims up to date.

Have some procedures for keeping track of such questions. Join local councils of voluntary service and read the local paper regularly so that you know what is going on. Join your national co-ordinating body so that you get news of developments in the field, both social and legal. Nominate one person to be responsible for keeping your subscriptions paid and your name on mailing lists.

Do people out there know about you?

Keeping in touch works in two directions. You must not only find out what other people are doing – you must also let them know what you are doing.

Do you have a handout which explains:

• your aims?
• your methods?
• your user group?
• who can refer?
• how referrals are made?
• opening times?

Do you have posters to advertise your services? When policies change do you let people know? Do you have a mailing list of who was sent your last handout so they get a copy of the changed version?

Do you use the facilities offered by your co-ordinating bodies to advertise to the field? Do you have a consistent style of presentation, a logo, even the same colour paper, so that people recognise your image? Do you ever contact the editor of your local paper? Do you make efforts to reach people? Are you prepared to speak in public?

Your work will affect the local community and other organisations. Avoid fund-raising strategies, for example, which stab other organisations in the back or which by their nature promise the impossible – at an amazingly cheap rate!

USING OUTSIDE HELP

11

Members of an organisation can do the exercises in this book without help from anyone trained in organisational skills. This way is less formal, less threatening and easier to arrange. People find their own solutions to the project's problems. But it is worth weighing up what you may gain from calling on outside help from someone who may be called a facilitator or a consultant.

Facilitators, and some consultants, help to set up the process by which members of the organisation can themselves find solutions to their problems. Other consultants would expect to be asked to report, usually in writing, with their diagnosis of the main problems, their causes and with recommended solutions. Such a consultant is given far more power to control the proceedings and to make recommendations for change.

Outside intervention helps to ensure that discussions are taken seriously. A facilitator enables those who normally feel responsible for the conduct of meetings or the future of the organisation to step down from their role for a while. A group with outside help is less likely to ramble off the point or refuse to face the real issue.

A facilitator can be especially helpful if some people involved find the idea of using exercises threatening. They might be alarmed because of the conflicts which they fear will be exposed, or simply because the whole thing is unfamiliar. A facilitator gives people confidence because they feel they are no longer so directly responsible for the success of discussions. They may also get the nerve to say things which otherwise they would not dare.

Some of the national co-ordinating federations for social or community work have fieldworkers prepared to help member organisations in this way. It would also be worth asking other organisations who have used a facilitator or consultant for recommendations.

Before an outsider is chosen, ensure that people in the organisation back the idea.

Be clear about the kind of help you need – for example, do you want long-term help with a consultant to look at relationships in the project? Then don't hire someone who specialises in setting up good organisational structures. Decide how you will choose the facilitator or consultant. Will all the essential people be involved, so that they have confidence in whoever is chosen?

Here are some useful questions to put to someone you are considering using:

- Do they charge per hour or per job and how much? How do they want to be paid?
- What are the most common problems they work with? What, in general terms, are their working methods?
- How much time do they have available? When would they be able to fit you in?
- What similar organisations have they worked with before and what was the outcome?

- Would they accept if they were asked in by one side in a dispute? For example, by a managing committee in conflict with workers, or vice versa?
- Do they accept that everything they are told is confidential?
- What support and supervision do they have?
- How would they like to get feedback from the organisation about their work?
- What procedures do they recommend for dealing with grievances that they and the organisation might have about each other?

Once someone has been chosen, it is essential to make sure that they are clear about their brief, and that they know enough about the work of the organisation, its aims and constraints, to be able to grasp the issues which will be discussed.

Ask the consultant or facilitator to explain their methods. Find out when the results will be available and decide how you plan to use them.

A clear contract between the organisation and the outside expert makes sure everyone knows where they stand. A review date should be agreed when the contract is made.

Below is an illustration of a basic contract.

The consultant agrees to:
Spend ten hours a week for four weeks observing interaction in meetings. Report on findings at the next meeting, and at the latest by 3.2.86 with practical suggestions in writing for improving teamwork.

The clients agree to:
Act as ordinarily as possible during observation.

Reject no practical suggestion the consultant makes without having discussed it sensibly.

Agreed by . . . .

Date . . . .

Date of review . . . .

Booklist

This booklist does not include everything that has been written. In particular, it includes very few of the standard textbooks on management and organisational theory. Readers who would like to know more should consult the helpful 'Guide to Further Study' in *Understanding Organisations* by Charles Handy, or the bibliography of any of the other textbooks we mention. We have tried to include books produced for community and self-help groups (some of these may unfortunately be out of print).

Assertiveness

BOWER, S. and BOWER, G. H. *Asserting Yourself: a practical guide for positive change*, Addison-Wesley, 1976.

FENSTERHEIM, H. and BAER, J. *Don't Say Yes When You Want to Say No*, Futura Publications, 1976.

Exercises and Games

BRANDES, D. and PHILLIPS, H. *Gamesters' Handbook: 140 games for teachers and group leaders*, Hutchinson, 1979.

DEACON, ESSER and MOORE. *Resource Manual for a Living Revolution* (an American book sometimes available at alternative bookshops).

HOPSON, B. and SCALLY, M. *Lifeskills Teaching Programmes*, McGraw Hill, 1980.

JELFS, M. *Manual for Action*, Action Resources Group, 1982.

PFEIFFER, J. W. and JONES, J. (eds). *A Handbook of Structured Experiences from Human Relations Training*, University Association Publishers and Consultants, Volume 1–1X, 1974–83.

PRIESTLY, P. *et al*. *Social Skills and Personal Problem Solving: a handbook of methods*, Tavistock Publications, 1978.

Finance

BLUME, H. *Fund Raising*, Routledge and Kegan Paul, 1977.

BLUME, H. and NORTON, M. *Accounting and Financial Management for Charities*, Directory of Social Change, 9 Mansfield Place, London NW3 1HS, 1980.

COMMUNITY ACCOUNTANCY PROJECT, *How to Manage Your Money, if you have any*, CAP, 34 Dalston Lane, London E8 3AZ, 2nd edn, 1984.

CYNOG-JONES, T. W. *Fundraising for and by small groups of volunteers*, Volunteer Centre Publications, 29 Lower Kings Road, Berkhamsted, Herts HP4 2AB, 1980.

DARNBOROUGH, A. and KINRADE, D. *Fundraising and Grant Aid: a practical and legal guide for charities and voluntary organisations*, Woodhead Faulkner, 8 Market Passage, Cambridge CB2 3PF, 1980.

FEEK, W. *Hitting the Right Notes*, National Youth Bureau, 17–23 Albion Street, Leicester LE1 6GD, 1982 (information on applying for funds).

JONES, M. (comp). *Government Grants: a guide for voluntary organisations*, Bedford Square Press/NCVO, 2nd edn, 1985.

NATIONAL ASSOCIATION FOR THE CARE AND RESETTLEMENT OF OFFENDERS, *Thoughts on Fundraising for Local Projects*, NACRO Publications, 169 Clapham Road, London SW9 0PU, undated.

SAMS, M. *The Role of the Budget. Drawing up the Budget. Using the Budget. Internal Controls*. Institute of Chartered Accountants in England and Wales, CHARTAC, PO Box 433, Moorgate Place, London EC2.

SMITH, J. *Basic Book-Keeping for Community Groups: a guide for treasurers*, London Voluntary Service Council, 68 Chalton Street, London NW1 1JR, 1979.

Legal

EDGINGTON, J. and BATES, S. *Legal Structures for Voluntary Organisations*, Bedford Square Press/NCVO, 1984.

LONGLEY, A. R., DOCKRAY, M. and SALLON, J. *Charity Trustees Guide*. Bedford Square Press/NCVO, 1982.

LONDON VOLUNTARY SERVICE COUNCIL. *Voluntary But Not Amateur: a Guide to the Law for Voluntary and Community Groups*. LVSC, 68 Chalton St, London NW1 1JR, 1980 (employing staff, handling money, being responsible for premises, constitutions, job contracts, organising public affairs, etc.).

NATIONAL COUNCIL FOR VOLUNTARY ORGANISATIONS. *Insurance Protection for Voluntary Organisations and Voluntary Workers*, NCVO, 1983.

PHILLIPS, A. and SMITH, K. *Charitable Status. A practical handbook*, Interchange, 15 Wilkin Street, London NW5 3NG, 2nd edn, 1982 (how to register as a charity and legal duties of charities).

Meetings

CITRINE, LORD. *ABC of Chairmanship*, National Council of Labour Colleges, 4th edn, 1982.

INDUSTRIAL SOCIETY. *Chairmanship and Discussion-leading*, Industrial Society, PO Box IBQ, Robert Hyde House, 48 Bryanston Square, London W1H 1BQ, 1977.

MOORE, M. *Law and Procedure of Meetings*, Sweet and Maxwell, 1979.

PERRY, P. J. C. *Hours into Minutes*, British Association for Commercial and Industrial Education, 16 Park Crescent, London W1N 4AP, 1979 (guide to committee documentation).

Monitoring

CROWE, I. *On Record: a guide to project monitoring*, NACRO Publications, 1978.

CROWE, I. *What's Needed? A guide to exploring and assessing needs*, NACRO Publications, 1978.

KEY, M., HUDSON, P. and ARMSTRONG, J. *Evaluation Theory and Community Work*, Community Projects Foundation, 60 Highbury Grove, London N5 2AG, 1976.

LONDON VOLUNTARY SERVICE COUNCIL. *Evaluation of Community Work*, LVSC, 68 Chalton Street, London NW1 1JR, 1978.

OPPENHEIM, A. N. *Questionnaire Design and Attitude Measurement*, Heinemann Educational Books, 1968.

SECORD, P. F. and BACKMAN, C. W. *Social Psychology*, McGraw-Hill Kogakusha, 1974.

Publicity

JONES, M. *Voluntary Organisations and the Media*, Bedford Square Press/NCVO, 1984.

MACSHANE, D. *Using the Media: How to deal with the press, television and radio*, Pluto Press, 1979 (practical guide plus directory).

WHISKIN, N. *Handling the Public Protest*, NACRO Publications, 1978.

Racism

BROWN, C. *Black and White Britain: the third PSI survey*, Heinemann, 1984.

CHEETHAM, J., PRESCOTT, W. et al. (eds). *Social and Community work in a Multi-Racial Society*, Harper and Row, 1982.

ELLIS, J. 'Management Committees and Race Equality: Anti-racism in the voluntary sector – a picture of inaction', *MDU Bulletin* No. 5 (supplement), NCVO, June 1985.

ETHNIC MINORITY UNIT, GREATER LONDON COUNCIL. *Anti-Racist Work in the Independent Voluntary Sector*, 1984. EMU, GLC, County Hall, London SE1 7PB.

JOHN, G. and PARKES, N. *Working with Black Youth: complementary or competing perspectives*, 1984. National Youth Bureau, 17–23 Albion Street, Leicester LE1 6GD.

KING'S FUND CENTRE. *An Experiment in Advocacy: the Hackney Multi-Ethnic Women's Health Project*, 1984. King's Fund Centre, 126 Albert Street, London NW1 7NJ.

MOODLEY, K. *An Anti-Racist Approach to the Care of Under Fives: some issues of principles, policy and practice*, Lewisham Borough Council, 1983.

NATIONAL ASSOCIATION OF CITIZENS ADVICE BUREAUX. *The Kirklees Ethnic Minorities Advice Project*, 1984. CAB Occasional paper 16, NACAB, 115 Pentonville Road, London N1 9LZ.

NATIONAL COUNCIL FOR VOLUNTARY ORGANISATIONS: *A Multi-Racial Society: the role of national voluntary organisations*, Bedford Square Press/ NCVO, 1984.

NATIONAL FEDERATION OF HOUSING ASSOCIATIONS. *Race and Housing: a guide for housing associations*, 1982; *Race and Housing: still a cause for concern*, 1985; *Ethnic Record Keeping and Monitoring*, 1985. NFHA, 175 Grays Inn Road, London WC1X 8UP.

OHRI, A. et al. (eds). *Community Work and Racism*, Routledge and Kegan Paul/Association of Community Workers, 1982.

SOUTHWARK COUNCIL FOR VOLUNTARY SERVICE. *Equal Opportunities: some steps towards race equality in employment* (short handbook with practical tips on equal opportunities employment procedures for voluntary organisations), SCVS, 135 Rye Lane, London SE15, 1984.

STARES, R. *Insights into Black Self Help*, Commission for Racial Equality, 1984.

Staffing

BRENT VOLUNTARY SERVICE COUNCIL. *Good Employment Practices in the Voluntary Sector*, Brent VSC, 74 Tubbs Road, London NW10 4RE, 1984.

COLLINSON, L. and HODKINSON, C. *Employment Law Keynotes*, Colgran Publications, 1985.

CRONER. *Guide to Fair Dismissal. Guide to Discipline. Guide to interviews.* Croner Publications, 1984 and 1985.

KUROWSKA, S. *Employing People in Voluntary Organisations*, Bedford Square Press/NCVO, 1984.

LANE, D. *Staffing Ratios in Residential Establishments*, Residential Care Association, 1980 (suggests formulae for calculating staffing levels).

MANPOWER SERVICES COMMISSION. *Code of Good Practice on the Employment of Disabled People*. MSC, Room W10, 30 Moorfoot, Sheffield S1 4PQ, 1984.

NATIONAL ASSOCIATION FOR THE CARE AND RESETTLEMENT OF OFFENDERS. *Appointing Staff: guidelines for project management committees*, NACRO Publications, 1978.

NATIONAL ASSOCIATION FOR THE CARE AND RESETTLEMENT OF OFFENDERS. *Induction Programmes for New Project Staff*, NACRO Publications, 1978.

NATIONAL ASSOCIATION OF VOLUNTARY HOSTELS. *Notes on Staffing Issues in Hostels*, NAVH, 33 Long Acre, London WC2E 9LA, 1981. (Staffing levels, organisation of staff teams, support, conditions of employment, relations with management and client participation in making decisions).

REDMAN, W. *Working with Volunteers 1. Support*, Volunteer Centre, 1977.

MURPHY, G. *Working with Volunteers 2. Training*, Volunteer Centre, 1977.

JOHNSTON, D. *Working with Volunteers 3. Recruitment and Selection*, Volunteer Centre, 1978.

Working Together

ASSOCIATION OF RESEARCHERS IN VOLUNTARY ACTION AND COMMUNITY INVOLVEMENT. *Management in Voluntary Organisations*. ARVAC, 26 Queens Road, Wivenhoe, Essex CO7 9JH, 1984.

BRANDOW, K., McDONNELL, J. and VOCATIONS FOR SOCIAL CHANGE. *No Bosses Here!: a manual on working collectively and co-operatively*, New Society Publishers, 4722 Baltimore Ave, Philadelphia, PA 1914, 2nd edn, 1984.

COOPER, S. and HEENAN, C. *Preparing, Designing and Leading Workshops: a humanistic approach*, CBI Publishing Co, 51 Sleeper Street, Boston, Massachusetts 02210, 1980.

DUHAN, T. and SOUTHGATE, J. *Making the Co-op Work*, Holloway Tenant Co-op, 107 Tollington Way, London N7 8LX, 1978 (an account of a training course and exercises with a housing co-op).

FREEMAN, J. *The Tyranny of Structurelessness*, Anarchist Workers Association, 13 Coltman Street, Hull HU3 2SG, 1970. (Reprint of a classic pamphlet on the problems of leaderless groups. Alternative bookshops are likely to know where you could find a reprint.)

GASKELL, G. and SEALY, P. *Groups. Social Psychology Block 13*, Open University Press, 1976.

HACKNEY COMMUNITY ACTION. *Community Groups Information Pack*, HCA, 380 Old Street, London EC1V 9LT, 1983.

HANDY, C. *Understanding Organisations*, Penguin Modern Management Texts, 1979 (basic textbook on organisation theory).

ISLINGTON VOLUNTARY ACTION COUNCIL. *Managing Voluntary Organisations and Small Groups*, IVAC, 309 Upper Street, London N1 2TU, 1984 (pamphlet).

MIND. *Development Papers. Guidelines on four areas of community self-help groups: operational, education/influential, fundraising, projects*, 1979. From MIND Bookshop, 155/7 Woodhouse Lane, Leeds LS2 3EF.

PARKINSON, C. N. *Parkinson's Law*, John Murray, 1958.

PITT, J. and KEANE, M. *Community Organising? You've Never Really Tried It. The Challenge to Britain from the USA*. J & P Publications, 318 High Street, Birmingham B17 9PU, 1984.

RANDALL, R., SOUTHGATE, J. and TOMLINSON, F. *Co-operative and Community Group Dynamics*, Barefoot Books, 12 Nassington Road, London NW3 2UD, 1980 (Reichian and Freire theories to explain task group processes).

RUBIN, I., PLOVNICK, M. and FRY, R. *Task Oriented Team Development*, Dale Loveluck Associates, 1976.

SMITH, J, and PEARSE, M. *Community Groups Handbooks: 1. Getting Involved. 2. Communities, Issues and Authorities. 3. Taking Action. 4. How Community Groups Work. 5. Community Action and Society*. Community Projects Foundation, 60 Highbury Grove, London N5 2AG, 1977.

STANTON, A. *Windows on Collective Working*. Department of Social Policy, School of Policy Studies, Cranfield Institute of Technology, Cranfield, Bedford MK43 0AL, 1984.

Miscellaneous

NATIONAL FEDERATION OF COMMUNITY ORGANISATIONS. *The Community Organisations Survival Kit*. NFCO, 8–9 Upper Street, London N1 0PQ, 1982.

UNELL, J. *Finding and Running Premises*, Bedford Square Press/NCVO, 1984.

WHITEHEAD, G. *Office Practice*. Made Simple Books, Heinemann, 1980.

WOLFENDEN, Sir John. *Future of Voluntary Organisations*. Croom Helm, 1977.

NCVO Information Sheets

The following sheets issued by NCVO Information Department are relevant (price 50p each including postage):

No. 17 *Selective Bibliography of Fundraising Books and Pamphlets*, 1985.

No. 20 *What is a Charity? Charity Law and Formation of Charities*, 1985.

No. 29 *How to Apply for a Grant*, 1985.

No. 31 *Honorary Officers and What They Do*, 1985.